4 - 38

5 95

HOW I USED TRUTH

By H. Emilie Cady

Unity Books
Unity Village, Missouri 64065

How I Used Truth was first published in 1916 under the title *Miscellaneous Writings*. Edition entitled *How I Used Truth* was published by Unity Books; seventeen printings through 1985. Revised edition, 1986.

Cover design by Lisa Bowser

Revised Edition ©1986 by
Unity School of Christianity
Unity Village, Missouri 64065

LLC: 85-051423
ISBN: 0-87159-056-5

DEDICATED

TO THE MANY LOVING FRIENDS ALL
OVER THE WORLD WHO HAVE BEEN
CHEERED AND HELPED BY THESE
SIMPLE MESSAGES.

Foreword

Because of repeated requests of many friends who have been helped by reading my various booklets and magazine articles, it seemed best to publish them all under one cover, to offer a convenient way for readers to have help always at hand. The papers that make up this volume have been written from time to time as a result of practical daily experience. In none of them is there anything occult or mysterious; neither has there been any attempt at literature. Each chapter is plain and simple.

In revising the articles, there have been a few nonessential changes; yet the principle and its application remain the same. Truth is that which is so, and it can never change. Every true statement here is as true and as workable today as it was when these papers were written. We ask no one to believe that which is here written simply because it is presented as Truth. "Prove all things" for yourself; it is possible to prove every statement in this book. Every statement given was proved before it was written. No person can solve another's problem. Each must work out his own salvation. Here are some effectual rules, suggestions, and helps; but results that one obtains from them will depend on how faithfully and persistently one uses the helps given.

I am grateful for the many words of appreciation that have come to me from time to time. These words are encouraging to one who is trying to solve her own life's problems, as you are trying to solve yours, by the teachings of the Master.

Lessons in Truth, because of its effective helpfulness, has been published in many languages, and in Braille for the blind. Let us hope that this book, now sent forth with the same objective—that of being a practical living help in daily life—may meet the same fate.

—H. Emilie Cady
January 1, 1916

CONTENTS

Why?

The following is a letter written by H. Emilie Cady to Lowell Fillmore. In this letter Doctor Cady says many helpful and inspiring things that we believe will be welcomed by those who read *How I Used Truth*.

Dear Mr. Fillmore:

When I sent you, a few weeks ago, a copy of the little pamphlet *All-Sufficiency in All Things*, which you said had been surreptitiously printed by an anonymous publisher, you wondered why I felt so keenly about the fact that the article had been broken up, put under different headings, and so forth. Let me tell you why.

1

Almost every one of the simply written articles in *How I Used Truth* was born out of the travail of my soul after I had been weeks, months, sometimes years, trying by affirmations, by claiming the promises of Jesus, and by otherwise faithfully using all of the knowledge of Truth that I then possessed to secure deliverance for myself or others from some distressing bondage that thus far had defied all human help.

One of these cases was that of my own old father, who, though perfectly innocent, had been kept in exile for five years; put there by the wicked machinations of another man. No process of law that I had invoked, no human help, not even the prayers that I had offered had seemed to avail for his deliverance. One day while sitting alone in my room, my hands busy with other things, my heart cried out, "O God, stretch forth Thy hand and deliver!" Instantly the answer came: "I have no hands but human hands. Your hand is my hand; stretch it forth spiritually and give whatsoever you will to whomsoever you will, and I will establish it."

Unquestioningly I obeyed. From that moment, without any further external help or striving, the way of his release was opened ahead of us more rapidly almost than we could step into it. Within a few days my dear father came home a free man, justified, exonerated, both publicly and privately, beyond anything we could have asked or thought.* Then I wrote *God's Hand.*

Another case was that of a dear young friend who had been placed in my care. He was just entering on a life of drinking and dissipation. There were weeks of awful anxiety, as I saw him drinking day by day, before I reached the place where I could "loose him, and let him go." When I did reach that place and stood there steadfastly (in spite of appearances), it required only a few hours to see him so fully healed that although forty years have passed, he has yet to touch a drop of liquor or indulge in any form of dissipation since that time. The lesson *Loose Him and Let Him Go* was then written.

Then came the question of money supply. I

*The case was written up by all the papers in the country in which my father resided as well as in the New York Sun. His innocence was clearly established. Once again he sat happily under the trees of his own dooryard and received congratulations. Delegation after delegation came from miles around; freinds who had known him from childhood came to assure him that his long life of uprightness had, in their minds, never been questioned. He was seventy-five years of age and, being an honest man, had felt the disgrace deeply. These staunch friends had been unable to help until God moved. The faith of many was renewed by his exoneration.

had a good profession with plenty of patients paying their bills monthly. But there were also other people coming to me daily for help, people whose visible means of support were gone. These cases of lack, as they presented themselves to me, were like cases of gnawing cancer or painful rheumatism. Therefore, there must be a way out through Truth, and I must find it. As always, instead of rushing to others for help in these tight places, I stayed at home within my own soul and asked God to show me the way. He did. He gave me the clear vision of Himself as *All-Sufficiency in All Things;* and then He said: "Now prove it, so that you can be of real help to the hundreds who do not have a profession or business on which to depend." From that day on, no ministry or work of any kind was ever done by me for "pay." No monthly bills were sent, no office charges made. I saw plainly that I must be working as God works, without expectation or thought of return. Free gift.

For more than two years I worked at this problem, never letting a human being know what I was trying to prove, for had He not said to me, "Prove me now herewith ... if I will not open you the windows of heaven, and pour you out a blessing, that there shall not be room enough *to receive it*"?

More than once in the ongoing the body was faint for want of food, and yet, so sure was I of what God had shown me that day after day I taught cheerfully and confidently to those who came to my office the Truth of God as the substance of all supply—and there were many in those days. At the end of two years of apparent failure I suddenly felt that I could not endure the privation any longer. Again, in near desperation from deferred hope of success, I went direct to God and cried out: "Why, why this failure? You told me in the vision that if I would give up the old way and trust to You alone, You would prove to me Your sufficiency. Why have You failed to do it?"

His answer came flashing back in these words: "God said, Let there be light: and there was light." It was all the answer He gave. At the moment I did not understand. I kept repeating it again and again, the words *God said* becoming more and more emphasized, until at last they were followed by the words "Without him [the Word] was not anything made that hath been made." That was all I needed. I saw plainly that while I had, for two years, hopefully and happily gone on enduring hardships believing that God would supply, I had not once spoken the word: *"It is done: God is now manifested as my supply."*

Believe me, that day I spoke the word of my deliverance. Suffice it to say that the supply problem was ended that day for all time and has never entered my life or mind since. This is the why of the article *The Spoken Word.*

I should like to give one more "Why" of *How I Used Truth.*

After days of excruciating pain from a badly sprained ankle, the ankle became enormously swollen, and it was impossible for me to attend to my professional work as an active medical practitioner. Ordinary affirmations of Truth were entirely ineffectual, and I soon struck out for the very highest statement of Truth that I could formulate. It was this: *There is only God; all else is a lie.* I vehemently affirmed it and steadfastly stuck to it. In twenty-four hours all pain and swelling—in fact, the entire "lie"—had disappeared. Out of this experience I wrote *Unadulterated Truth.*

Can you not see, dear Mr. Fillmore, how it is that these simply written articles in *How I*

Used Truth are as my children, and how all revision or changing of them seems to me like a violation of something sacred between God and me? I am sure you can. In each case I had proved God before I wrote. I thank the Fillmores that they have kept these messages just as they were written.

Yours in His name,
H. Emilie Cady

Finding the Christ in Ourselves

Throughout all His teaching Jesus tried to show those who listened to Him how He was related to the Father, and to teach them that they were related to the same Father in exactly the same way. Over and over He tried in different ways to explain to them that God lived within them, that He was: *"... not God of the dead, but of the living."* (Matt. 22:32) And never once did He assume to do anything of Himself, always saying: *"... I do nothing on my own authority...."* (John 8:28) *"... The Father who dwells in me does his works."* (John 14:10) But it was very hard then for people to understand, just as it is very hard for us to understand today.

8

There were, in the person of Jesus, two distinct regions. There was the fleshly, mortal part that was Jesus, the son of man; then there was the central, living, real part that was Spirit, the Son of God—that was the Christ, the Anointed. So each one of us has two regions of being—one the fleshly, mortal part, which feels its weakness and insufficiency, saying, "I can't." Then at the very center of our being there is a something that, in our highest moments, knows itself more than conqueror over all things; it always says, "I can, and I will." It is the Christ child, the Son of God, the Anointed in us. *"And call no man your father on earth,"* said Jesus, *"for you have one Father, who is in heaven."* (Matt. 23:9)

He who created us did not make us and set us apart from Himself, as a workman makes a table or a chair and puts it away as something completed and only to be returned to the maker when it needs repairing. Not at all. God not only created us in the beginning, but He is the very fountain of life abiding within us. From this fountain constantly springs new life to recreate our mortal bodies. He is the ever-abiding intelligence that fills and renews our minds. His creatures would not exist a moment were He to be, or could He be, separated from them. ... *We are the temple of the living God; as God said, "I will live in them and move among them...."* (II Cor. 6:16)

Let us suppose that a beautiful fountain is supplied from some hidden but inexhaustible source. At its center it is full of strong, vigorous life, bubbling up continually with great activity, but at the outer edge the water is so nearly motionless as to have become impure and covered with scum. This exactly represents man. He is composed of a substance infinitely more subtle, more real than water. *" '... We are indeed his offspring.' "* (Acts 17:28) Man is the offspring—or the springing forth into visibility—of God the Father. At the center he is pure Spirit, made in the image and likeness of the Father, substance of the Father, one with the Father, fed and renewed continually from the inexhaustible good, which is the Father. *" 'In him we live and move and have our being.' "* (Acts 17:28) At the outer edge, where stagnation has taken place (which is man's body), there is not much that looks Godlike in any way. We get our eyes fixed on the circumference, or external of our being. We lose consciousness of the indwelling, ever-active, unchanging God at the center, and we see ourselves sick, weak, and in every way miserable. It is not until we learn to live at the center and to know that we have power to radiate from that center this unceasing, abundant life, that we are well and strong.

Jesus kept His eyes away from the external altogether, and kept His thoughts at the central part of His being, which was the Christ. *"Do not judge by appearances,"* He said, that is, according to the external, *"but judge with right judgment"* (John 7:24) according to the real truth, or judge from Spirit. In Jesus, the Christ, or the central spark that was God, the same that lives in each of us today, was drawn forth to show itself perfectly, over and above the body, or fleshly man. He did all His mighty works, not because He was given some greater or different power from that which God has given us—not because He was a Son of God and we only children of God— but because this same divine spark, which the Father has implanted in every child, had been fanned into a bright flame by His prenatal influences, early surroundings, and by His own later efforts in holding Himself in constant, conscious communion with the Father, the Source of all love, life, and power.

To be tempted does not mean to have things come to you which, however much they may affect others, do not affect you, because of some superiority in you. It means to be tried, to suffer, and to have to make effort to resist. Hebrews speaks of Jesus as: *... one who in every respect has been tempted as we are* .... (Heb. 4:15) And Jesus Himself confessed to having been tempted when He said to His disciples: *"You are those who have continued with me in my trials* ...." (Luke 22:28) The humanity of the Nazarene "suffered being tempted," or tried, just as much as you and I suffer today because of temptations and trials, and in exactly the same way.

We know that during His public ministry Jesus spent hours each day alone with God. None of us knows what He went through in the years of His early manhood—just as you and I are doing today—in overcoming the mortal, His fleshly desires, His doubts and fears, until He came into the perfect recognition of this indwelling Presence, this "Father in me," to whom He ascribed the credit for His wonderful works. He had to learn as we are having to learn; He had to hold fast as we are having today to hold fast; He had to try

over and over to overcome, as we are doing, or else He was not "in every respect"
tempted as we are.

We all must recognize that it was the
Christ within that made Jesus what He was;
and our power now to help ourselves and to
help others lies in our comprehending the
truth—for it is a truth, whether we realize it
or not—that this same Christ that lived in
Jesus lives within us. It is the part of Himself
that God has put within us, which ever lives
there with an inexpressible love and desire to
spring to the circumference of our being, or to
our consciousness, as our sufficiency in all
things. *The Lord, your God, is in your midst,
a warrior who gives victory; he will rejoice
over you with gladness, he will renew you in
his love; he will exult over you with loud singing . . . .* (Zeph. 3:17) Christ within us is the
"beloved Son," the same as it was in Jesus. It
is the "I in them, and thou in me, that they
may be perfected" of which Jesus spoke.

In all this explanation we would detract
nothing from Jesus. He is still our Savior,
in that He went through unutterable suffering, through the perfect crucifixion of self,
that He might lead us to God; that He might
show us the way out of our sin, sickness, and

trouble; that He might manifest the Father to us and teach us how this same Father loves us and lives in us. We love Jesus and must ever love Him with a love that is greater than all others, and to prove our love, we would follow His teachings and His life closely. In no way can we do this perfectly, except by trying to get at the real meaning of all that He said, and letting the Father work through us as He did through Him, our perfect Elder Brother and Savior.

Jesus sometimes spoke from the mortal part of Himself, but He lived so almost wholly in the Christ part of Himself, so consciously in the center of His being, where the very essence of the Father was bubbling up in ceaseless activity, that He usually spoke from that part.

When He said: *"Come to me . . . and I will give you rest"* (Matt. 11:28) He could not have meant to invite humankind to come unto His personal, mortal self, for He knew of the millions of men and women who could never reach Him. He was then speaking from the Christ self of Him, meaning not "Come to me, Jesus," but "come to the Christ"; nor did He mean, "Come to the Christ living in me," for comparatively few could ever do that. But

He said: "... *The words that I say to you I do not speak on my own authority; but the Father who dwells in me does his works.*" (John 14:10) Then it was the Father saying not "Come to Jesus," but "Come to me"; that is, "Come up out of the mortal part of you where all is sickness and sorrow and trouble, into the Christ part where I dwell, and I will give you rest. Come up into the realization that you are one with the Father, that you are surrounded and filled with divine love, that there is nothing in the universe that is real but the good, and that all good is yours, and it will give you rest."

"No one comes to the Father, but by me" (John 14:6) does not mean that God is a stern Father whom we must coax and conciliate by going to Him through Jesus, His kinder, more easily entreated Son. Did not Jesus say: "... *He who has seen me has seen the Father* ..." (John 14:9) or in other words, "As I am in love and gentleness and accessibility, so is the Father"? These words mean that no one can come to the Father except through the Christ part of himself. You cannot come around through some other person or by any outside way. Another may teach you how to come, and assure you of all that is yours if

you do come, but you must retire within your own soul, find the Christ there, and look to the Father through the Son, for whatever good thing you may need.

Jesus was always trying to get the minds of the people away from His personality, and to fix them on the Father in Him as the source of His power. And when toward the last they were clinging to His mortal self, because their eyes had not yet been opened to understand about the Christ within their own souls, He said: "*... it is to your advantage that I go away, for if I do not go away, the Counselor will not come to you....*" (John 16:7) If He remained where they could keep looking to His personality, they would never know that the same Spirit of truth and power lived within them.

There is a great difference between a Christian life and a Christ life. To live a Christian life is to follow the teachings of Jesus, with the thought that God and Christ are wholly outside of us, to be called on but not always to answer. To live a Christ life is to follow Jesus' teachings in the knowledge that God's indwelling presence, which is always life, love, and power within us, is now ready and waiting to flow forth abundantly, lavishly into our consciousness and through us to others, the moment we open ourselves to it and trustfully expect it. One is a following after Christ, which is beautiful and good so far as it goes, but is always imperfect; the other is a letting Christ, the perfect Son of God, be manifested through us. One is an expecting to be saved sometime from sin, sickness, and trouble; the other is a knowing that we are, in reality, saved now from all these errors by the indwelling Christ, and by faith affirming it until the evidence is manifested in our bodies.

Simply believing that Jesus died on the Cross to appease God's wrath never saved and can never save anyone from present sin, sickness, or want, and was not what Jesus taught. "The demons also believe and shudder," we are told, but they are not saved thereby. There must be something more than this, a living touch of some kind, a sort of inter-sphering of our own soul with the divine Source of all good and giving. We are to have faith in the Christ, believe that the Christ lives in us and is God's Son in us; that this indwelling One has power to save and make us whole; even more, that He has made us whole already. For did not the Master say:

". . . Whatever you ask in prayer, you will receive, if you have faith"? (Matt. 21:22)

If, then, you are manifesting sickness, you are to ignore the seeming—which is the external, or circumference of the pool where the water is stagnant and the scum has risen—and, speaking from the center of your being, say: "This body is the temple of the living God; the Lord is now in His holy temple; Christ in me is my life; Christ is my health; Christ is my strength; Christ is perfect. Therefore, I am now perfect, because He dwells in me as perfect life, health, strength." Say these words with all earnestness, trying to realize what you are saying, and almost immediately the perennial fountain of life at the center of your being will begin to bubble up and continue with rapidly increasing activity, until new life will radiate through pain, sickness, sores, all diseases, to the surface, and your body will show forth the perfect life of Christ.

Suppose it is money that you need. Take the thought, "Christ is my abundant supply. He is here within me now, and greatly desires to manifest Himself as my supply. His desires are fulfilled now." Do not let your thoughts run off into how He is going to do it, but just hold steadily to the thought of the supply here and now, taking your eyes off all other sources, and He will surely honor your faith by manifesting Himself as your supply a hundredfold more abundantly than you have asked or thought. So also with "whatever you ask in prayer." But remember the earnest words of James, the Apostle: ... *he who doubts is like a wave of the sea that is driven and tossed by the wind. For that person must not suppose that a double-minded man, unstable in all his ways, will receive anything from the Lord.* (James 1:6-8)

Nowhere in the New Testament is the thought conveyed that Jesus came that there might be, after death, a remission of the penalty for sin. That belief is a pure fiction of our ignorant, carnal minds. In many places in the Bible, reference is made to "remission of sins." According to Luke, Jesus said that repentance and ... remission of sins should be preached in His name unto all the nations.

"Sins," in the original text, does not mean crime deserving punishment. It means any mistake or failure that brings suffering. Jesus came that there might be remission or cessation of sins, of wrongs, of mistakes, which were inevitably followed by suffering.

He came to bring: "... *good news of a great joy which will come to all the people* ...." (Luke 2:10) News of what? News of salvation. When? Where? Not salvation from punishment after death, but salvation from mistakes and failures here and now. He came to show us that God, our Creator and Father, longs to be to us, through the Christ, the abundance of all things that we need or desire. But our part is to choose to have Him and then follow His admonition to "hold fast till I come"—not till He comes after death, but until He manifests Himself. For instance, in looking to Him for health, when by an act of your will you stop looking to any material source (and this is not always easy to do) and declare the Christ in you to be the only life of the body and always perfect life, you need only to hold steadfastly, without wavering, to the thought, in order to become well.

When once you have put matter into the hands of the indwelling, ever-present Christ, in whom there is at all times an irrepressible desire to spring to our rescue and to do all things for us, do not dare to take it back into your mortal hands again to work out for yourself, for by so doing you simply put off the time of His bringing it to pass. All you have to do in the matter is to hold to the thought, "It is done. It is manifest now." This divine Presence is our sufficiency in all things, and will materialize itself as such in whatever we need or desire, if we but trustfully expect it.

This matter of trusting the Christ within to do all things for us—realizing that we are one with Christ and that to Christ is given all power—is not something that comes to any of us spontaneously. It comes by persistent effort. We begin by determining that we will trust Him as our deliverance, as our health, our riches, our wisdom, our all, and we keep on by a labored effort, until we form a spiritual habit. No habit bursts full-grown into our lives, but comes from a succession of little acts. When you see anyone doing the works of Christ, healing the sick, loosing the bound, and so forth, by the word of Truth spoken in faith, you may be sure that this faith did not come to him from some outside source all at once. If you knew the facts, you would probably know of days and nights when with clenched fists and set teeth the person held fast to the Christ within, "trusting where they could not trace," until he found himself possessing the very "faith of Jesus."

If we want the Father within, which is the Christ, to manifest as all things through us, we must learn to keep the mortal of us still, to still all its doubts and fears and false beliefs, and to hold rigidly to the Christ only. In His name we may speak the words of healing, of peace, and of deliverance to others, but as Jesus said of Himself, so we must also say of ourselves: "*. . . I do nothing on my own authority . . .*" (John 8:28) and: "*. . . the Father who dwells in me does his works.*" (John 14:10) He is the ever-present power to overcome all errors, sickness, weakness, ignorance, or whatever they may be. We claim this power, or bring it into our consciousness where it is of practical use, by declaring over and over that it is ours already. Saying and trying to realize, "Christ is my wisdom, therefore I know Truth," will in a short time make us understand spiritual things better than months of study. Our saying *"Christ is my strength, I cannot be weak or frail,"* will make us strong enough to meet any emergency with calm assurance.

Remember, we do not begin by feeling these things at first, but by earnestly and faithfully saying them, and acting as though they were true—and this is the faith that brings the power into manifestation.

The Christ lives in us always. God, the creative energy, sent His Son first, even before the body was formed, and He ever abides within: ... *the first-born of all creation* .... (Col. 1:15) But it is with us as it was with the ship on the tempestuous sea after the storm arose: Jesus' being in the vessel did not keep it from rocking, or the angry waves from beating against it, for He was asleep. It was only after He was awakened and brought out to manifest His power that the sea became still and the danger was over.

The Christ in us has been there all the time, but we have not known it, and so our little ships have been tossed about by sickness and poverty and distrust until we have seemed almost lost. I, the true spiritual self of me, am one with the Christ. You, the true spiritual self of you, are one with the Christ. The true self of every person is the child of God, made in His image. *Beloved, we are God's children now; it does not yet appear what we shall be, but we know that when he appears we shall be like him, for we shall see him as he is.* (I John 3:2) Now, already, we are sons. When He shall appear—not when, sometime after the transition called death, He, some great, glorious Being, shall burst into view, but when we have learned to still the mortal of us, and let the Father manifest at our surface, through the indwelling Christ—then we shall be like Him, for He only will be visible through us.

See what love the Father has given us, that we should be called children of God; and so we are. (I John 3:1) We are not simply reflections or images of God, but expressions (from *ex,* out of, and *premere,* to press or force), hence a forcing out of God, the All-Good, the All-Perfect. We are projections of the invisible presence into visibility. God made us one with the Father, even as Jesus was, and just in proportion as we recognize this fact and claim our birthright, the Father in us will be manifested to the world.

Most of us innately avoid saying, "Thy will be done." Because of false teaching, and from associations, we have believed that this prayer, if answered, would take away from us all that gives us joy or happiness. Surely nothing could be further from the truth. Oh, how we have tried to crowd the broad love of God into the narrow limits of human mind! The grandest, most generous, loving father that ever lived is but the least bit of God's fatherhood manifested through the flesh. God's will for us means more love, more purity, more power, more joy in our lives every day.

No study of spiritual or material things, no effort, though it be superhuman on our part, could ever be as effectual in making grand, Godlike creatures, showing forth the same limitless soul that Jesus showed, as just praying continually the one prayer, "Thy will be done"; for the Father's will is to manifest His perfect Being through us. *Among the creatures, one is better than another, according as the Eternal Good manifesteth itself and worketh more in one than in another. Now that creature in which Eternal Good most manifesteth itself, shineth forth, worketh, is most known and loved, is the best; and that wherein the Eternal Good is least manifested, is least of all creatures.* (Theologia Germanica)

For in him all the fulness of God was pleased to dwell . . . (Col. 1:19) fullness of love, fullness of life, fullness of joy, of power, of All-Good. Christ is in us, one with us, so we may boldly and with confidence say, "In Christ all things are mine." Declaring it will make it manifest.

Above all things else, learn to keep to the Christ within yourself, not that within someone else. Let the Father manifest through you in His own way, though His manifestation differs from that in His other children. Heretofore even the most spiritually enlightened of us have been mere pygmies, because we have, by the action of our conscious thought, limited the divine manifestation to make it conform to the manifestation through someone else. God will make of us spiritual giants if we will but take away all limits and give Him opportunity.

Although it be good and profitable that we should learn and know what great and good men have wrought and suffered, and how God hath dealt with them, and wrought in them and through them, yet it were a thousand times better that we should in ourselves learn and perceive and understand who we are, how and what our own life is, what God is doing in us, and what He will have us do. (Theologia Germanica)

All the blessings promised in the twenty-eighth chapter of Deuteronomy are to those who: ... *hearken diligently unto my commandments* .... (Deut. 11:13, A.V.) This means those who seek the inner voice in their own souls and learn to listen to and obey what it says to them individually, regardless of what it says to any other person, no matter how far he or she may be advanced in spiritual understanding. This voice will not lead you exactly as it leads any other, but, in the infinite variety, there will be perfect harmony, for there is but *one God and Father of us all, who is above all and through all and in all.* (Eph. 4:6)

Ralph Waldo Emerson says: *Every soul is not only the inlet but may become the outlet of all there is in God.* We can only be this by keeping ourselves consciously in open communication with God without the intervention of any other person between God and us. "*... The anointing which you received from him abides in you, and you have no need that any one should teach you ....*" (I John 2:27) *"But the Counselor, the Holy Spirit, whom the Father will send in my name, he will teach you all things ...."* (John 14:26)

"When the Spirit of truth comes, he will guide you into all the truth; for he will not speak on his own authority, but whatever he hears he will speak, and he will declare to you the things that are to come." (John 16:13)

It needs but the one other little word *now,*

firmly and persistently held in the mind, to bring into manifestation through us the highest ideal that we are capable of forming; far higher, for does it not say: "... *as the heavens are higher than the earth, so are my ways higher than your ways and my thoughts than your thoughts*"? (Isa. 55:9) This manifestation through us will be the fulfillment of God's ideal, instead of our limited, mortal ideal, when we learn to let Spirit lead and to hold our conscious mind to the now.

You want to manifest the perfect Christ. Affirm with all your heart and soul and strength that you do so manifest now, that you manifest health and strength and love and Truth and power. Let go the notion of being or doing anything in the future. God knows no time but the eternal now. You can never know any other time, for there is no other. You cannot live an hour or ten minutes in the future. You cannot live it until you reach it, and then it becomes the now. Saying or believing salvation and deliverance are to be, will forever, and through all the eternal ages, keep them just a little ahead of you, always to be reached but never quite realized.

Now is the acceptable time; behold, now is the day of salvation, (II Cor. 6:2) said Paul.

He said nothing about our being saved from our distresses after death, but always taught present salvation. God's work is finished in us now. All the fullness abides in the indwelling Christ now. Whatever we persistently declare is done now, is manifested now, we shall see fulfilled.

Neither Do I Condemn Thee

Few of us have any idea of the destructive potency of condemnatory words or thoughts. Even among Truth students who know the power of the spoken word—and because they know it, so much greater is that power—there is a widespread tendency to condemn the churches and all orthodox Christians, to criticize and speak disparingly of students of different schools (as though there could be only one school of Christ), and even to discuss among themselves the failings of individuals who, in ways differing from their own, earnestly seek the Christ.

Let us stop and see what we are doing. Why should we condemn the churches? Did not

Jesus teach in the synagogues? He did not withdraw from the church and speak contemptuously of it. No, He remained in it, trying to show people wherein they were making mistakes, trying to lead them up to a higher view of God as their Father, and to stimulate them to live more truly righteous lives. If Jesus found hypocrisy in the churches, He did not content Himself with saying, "I am holier than thou," but remained with them and taught them a more excellent way: that the inside of the platter must be made clean.

Is the servant greater than his Lord? Shall not we, whom the Father has called into such marvelous light, rather help those sitting in darkness, even in the churches, than utter one word of condemnation against them? A loyal son or daughter does not condemn his or her father or mother because in their day and generation, with the limitations of their day, they did not grow to his or her present standard. We do not condemn the tallow candle or the stagecoach because we have grown into a knowledge of electricity and steam power. We only see that out of the old grew the new, and that the old was necessary to the new.

God, in His eternal purposes, is carrying every living person on toward a higher

knowledge of the Truth, a more perfect
evolvement of Himself through the soul. If
some are being pushed on into the light of
Truth and consequent liberty more rapidly
than others, shall they turn and rend those
who are walking more slowly but just as surely toward the perfect light? No; but let them,
praising God for the marvelous revelation of
Himself within their own souls, lift up rather
than condemn any who are struggling toward
the light. Let them become workers together
with God, doers of the law, not judges.

Let no one who has been born into a knowledge of God dare to speak or even think disparagingly of or to anyone who is seemingly
behind him in spiritual growth, lest by so doing he be found working against God, who is
infinite wisdom as well as love.

Jesus said to the disciples, after they had
come into the consciousness of their oneness
with the Father by receiving the Holy Spirit:
*"If you forgive the sins of any, they are
forgiven; if you retain the sins of any, they are
retained."* (John 20:23) With what mighty
meaning these words are fraught, in this new
light that God has given us! See how our
speaking, even our very thinking, of the sins
or mistakes of others tends to fasten those

mistakes on them as realities.

Strong thoughts of condemnation about anyone by any person will give him the physical sensation of having been hit in the pit of the stomach with a stone. If he does not immediately throw off the feeling—as he can easily do by looking to the Father and saying over and over until it becomes reality, *"God, approve of me"*—it will destroy his consciousness of perfect life, and he will fall into a belief of weakness and discouragement more quickly than from any other cause.

We read that the eyes of God are too pure to behold iniquity. A pure person sees no licentiousness in another. A pure person sees no falsity in another. Perfect love responds not to envy, or fear, or jealousy in another. It "thinks no evil." Jesus said: *". . . the ruler of this world is coming. He has no power over me . . . ."* (John 14:30) So, unless there is something within us that responds to sin in others we shall not see it in them. *". . . By your words you will be justified, and by your words you will be condemned."* (Matt. 12:37) The moment we begin to criticize or condemn another, we prove ourselves guilty of the same fault to which we are giving cognizance.

All condemnation springs from looking at

personality. Personality (Latin, *persona*, a mask) is the outward appearance, not the real self. That anyone utters a word of condemnation of another is the surest proof that he is yet living largely in the external of his being, the personality; that he has not yet risen beyond the plane of those to whom the pure Nazarene said: *"Let him who is without sin among you be the first to throw a stone...."* (John 8:7) Just in proportion as we return to God, as we withdraw from the external to the within of ourselves, keeping our thoughts centered on Him who is perfect, shall we lose sight of personality, of divisions and differences, and become conscious of our oneness with one another and our oneness with God, our Father.

We are one always and forever, whether or not we realize it. Knowing this, you will see a new meaning in the words: *"Judge not that you be not judged. For with the judgment you pronounce you will be judged...."* (Matt. 7:1)

"For God sent the Son into the world, not to condemn the world, but that the world might be saved through him." (John 3:17) Yet when Philip said to Jesus: *"Lord, show us the Father, and we shall be satisfied,"* (John 14:8)

Jesus replied: "*. . . He who has seen me has seen the Father . . . .*" (John 14:9) Then, if God does not condemn, shall we, dare we, even in the smallest things? To each of us the Master says, "What is that to thee? Follow me."

Not while we are looking at the imperfect either in ourselves or in our brother, but while we *. . . beholding the glory of the Lord, are being changed into his likeness from one degree of glory to another; for this comes from the Lord who is the Spirit.* (II Cor. 3:18)

In His Name

Has it ever occurred to you that you almost daily take God's name in vain? Unless you are very watchful, very careful, you do so.

When God called Moses to lead the Children of Israel out of Egypt... *Moses said to God, "If I come to the people of Israel and say to them, 'The God of your fathers has sent me to you,' and they ask me, 'What is his name?' what shall I say to them?"*

God said to Moses, "I AM WHO I AM." And he said, "Say this to the people of Israel, 'I AM has sent me to you.'"

"... This is my name for ever, and thus I am to be remembered throughout all generations." (Exod. 3:13-15)

"I AM" is God's name. Every time you say, "I am sick," "I am weak," "I am discouraged," you are speaking God's name in vain.

I AM cannot be sick; I AM cannot be weary, or faint, or powerless; for I AM is all-life, all-power, All-Good.

"I AM," spoken with a downward tendency, is always false, always "in vain." A commandment says: *You shall not take the name of the Lord your God in vain; for the Lord will not hold him guiltless who takes his name in vain.* " (Exod. 20:7) And Jesus said: "*. . . by your words you will be justified, and by your words you will be condemned.*" (Matt. 12:37)

If you speak the "I AM" falsely, you will get the result of false speaking. If you say, "I am sick," you will get sickness; if you say, "I am poor," you will get poverty; for the law is: *. . . whatever a man sows, that he will also reap.* (Gal. 6:7) "I AM," spoken upward, toward the good, the true, is sure to outpicture in visible good, in success, in happiness.

Does all this sound foolish to you? Do you doubt that such power goes with the speaking of God's name? If so, just go alone, close you eyes, and in the depth of your own soul say over and over the name "I AM." Soon you will find your whole being filled with a sense of power that you never had before—power to overcome, power to accomplish, power to do all things.

I am because Thou art. I am what Thou art. I am one with Thee, O Thou infinite I AM! I am good. I am holy. I am well. I am, because Thou art.

The name of the Lord is a strong tower; the righteous man runs into it and is safe. (Prov. 18:10) They who think rightly about the power of the I AM spoken upward, simply have to run into it, as into a strong tower or fortress, and they are safe.

Did you ever go into a meeting where the "testimonies" given were the "I AM" spoken upward—"I am happy to be here," "I am glad I am a Christian," "I am hoping and trusting in God," and so forth? Attend such a gathering, and almost before you know it, you will find yourself lifted above your troubles and anxieties. You leave such a meeting with a feeling of joy and lightness, and a consciousness that you have the power to overcome all troubles and worries; you go, singing and confident, toward the very thing which an hour before seemed about to consume you.

Dear friends, you who at times feel discouraged, you who are continually irritated by the petty worries and anxieties of life, try for one week saying "I AM" upward, toward the good. Instead of saying, "I am afraid it will rain," say "I hope it will not rain"; instead of "I am sorry," say "I would have been glad had it been so and so"; instead of saying, "I am weak and cannot accomplish," say, "I am, because Thou art; I can accomplish, because I am." You will be astonished at the result.

The Christ, speaking through Jesus, said to the Jews who were boasting of being descendants of Abraham: *"Truly, truly, I say to you, before Abraham was, I am."* (John 8:58) And Paul, writing to Timothy, said: *"Let every one who names the name of the Lord depart from iniquity."* (II Tim. 2:19) Let every one who speaks the "I AM" keep it separated from iniquity, or from false speaking. Let it be spoken always upward, never downward. Jesus also said: *". . . if you ask anything of the Father, he will give it to you in my name."* (John 16:23) That is, in the name I AM. Whenever you desire—not supplicate, but desire, speaking the "I AM" upward—He will give what you ask. Every time you say, "I am happy," you ask in His name for happiness. Every time you say, "I am unhappy," you ask in His name for unhappiness. *"Hitherto,"* He said to the disciples, *"you have asked nothing in my name; ask, and you will receive, that your joy may be full."* (John 16:24) Is not this the trouble? Previously, what have we been asking in His name? Have we been asking for health or for sickness, for happiness or for unhappiness, for riches or for poverty, by the manner of our speaking the name I AM?

Have we spoken it upward, toward the good, or downward toward the not good? That which we have been receiving will tell the story. Jesus said that if they asked rightly in His name, their *"joy may be made full."* Is your joy full? If not, then give heed to your asking.

The disciples healed "in the name of Jesus Christ." In the name of Jesus Christ is the name of the I AM.

Suppose that a messenger is sent out from the executive mansion in Washington to do certain things in the name of the President of the United States. These three little words, "In his name," invest the messenger with the full power of the President, so far as the performing of that service is concerned.

In writing to the Colossians, Paul said: *And whatever you do, in word or deed, do everything in the name of the Lord Jesus, giving thanks to God the Father through him.* (Col. 3:17) Whatever we do heartily and sincerely in the name of Christ or the I AM carries with it the power of the I AM to accomplish—a power from a higher source, as the presidential messenger receives his power from a higher source. All power is given to Christ. Doing all things "in his name" puts aside our mortal personality and lets the Christ do the work. When Moses, with a sense of his personal insufficiency for so great a work, shrank from it, saying: *"Oh, my Lord, I am not eloquent... I am slow of speech and of tongue,"* (Exod. 4:10) Jehovah said to him: *"Who has made man's mouth?... Is it not I, the Lord? Now therefore go, and I will be with your mouth and teach you what you shall speak."* (Exod. 4:11, 12)

In Edward Everett Hale's story, "In His Name," a story in a setting of seven hundred years ago, it is no fairy tale that invests the words "In His Name" with such magic power. This little password carried safely, through the most dangerous places, all who went on errands of good. Locked doors were readily opened at the sound of the words. Soldier, sentry, officer of the guard, all gave way respectfully and instantly before it. Men were willing to leave their homes at a moment's notice and plunge into the greatest hardships "in His name."

Ministering today in His name, I say to you, troubled one, anxious one, weary one: Be strong! Be of good courage! Be hopeful! The world—the mortal—is overcome already. The Christ, the I AM, speaking through Jesus, has spoken, saying: "I have overcome the world."

" *'To him who conquers* (that is, to him who recognizes that already the world is overcome by the I AM, that there is nothing in all the universe but the I AM) *I will give some of the hidden manna, and I will give him a white stone, with a new name written on the stone which no one knows except him who receives it.'* " (Rev. 2:17)

"He who conquers, I will make him a pillar in the temple of my God; never shall he go out of it, and I will write on him the name of my God . . ." (Rev. 3:12) even the name I AM.

Loose Him and Let Him Go

One of the natural tendencies of the mortal mind is toward proselyting.

The moment we believe something to be true we begin to try to convert others to our belief. In our eagerness we forget that Truth is kaleidoscopic in its forms. We learn to say, with some degree of realization, "God works in me to will and to work for His good pleasure," but we quite forget that the same God is working equally in our brother "to will and to work."

Among the wise sayings of the ancient philosopher, Epictetus, we find these words: *Does any one bathe hastily? Do not say that he does it ill, but hastily. Does any one drink*

*much wine? Do not say that he does ill, but
that he drinks a great deal. For unless you
perfectly understand his motives, how should
you know if he acts ill? Thus you will not risk
yielding to any appearances but such as you
fully comprehend.*

Every person has an inherent right to freedom of choice, a right to live his life in his own way. One of the surest signs that a person is no longer in bondage himself is his willingness to give others their freedom, to allow others the privilege of seeking and finding God as they will.

Our great basic statement is "All is good, because all is God." In other words, God is the only intelligence, the only life at the center of every form of existing life. We say that we believe the highest manifestation of God is in humankind; that God ever abides at the center of all people, and is always in process of manifesting more and more of Himself, pure intelligence, perfect love, through our consciousness until we come to be consciously one with the Father in all things.

Do you believe this statement? If you believe it, where is there any cause for anxiety that you feel about your loved ones who are not, as you say, "in the Truth"?

If we truly believe that "all is good," we should not be troubled about those who apparently are going wrong. They may be going wrong according to our limited conception of right and wrong. But my brother, my sister, you are not your brother's keeper. He that will redeem, indeed, He that has already redeemed your brother or sister lives within him. The Christ, who ever loves at the center of every soul, ... *will neither slumber nor sleep.* (Psalms 121:4) God works in others, to bring them to themselves just as much as He is working in you and in me. We have absolutely nothing to fear about the eventual success of this worker. God never fails.

You have perhaps come to the flowering of the fruiting season, in your growth out of the darkness of sense belief into the light of spiritual understanding. It is blessed and beautiful to be where you are, and it is hard to human belief to see those whom you love just barely showing their heads above the earth of sin and mistake, further away from your conception of the good than ever before.

But here is the place for us to cling faithfully and trustingly to our basic statement. Paul said: ... *in this hope we were saved. Now hope that is seen is not hope....* (Rom.

8:24) Faith is not sight. Is our basic statement, "All is good," founded on Principle or on evidence of the senses? If on Principle, then it is immutable, unchangeable. And God is just as surely abiding at the center of your loved husband or son, working in him, when he is going down, as when he is coming up.

God is just as much the life of the seed when it is being planted in the dark earth, where, to the human sense, it is dead and all is lost, as He is the life of the new leaf which a few days later bursts into sight. In fact, it is because God is there at the center, working in the stillness, unseen, and not at all because of the fussy, noisy outside work that you and I do, that the seed comes forth into newness of life.

"Unless a grain of wheat falls into the earth and dies, it remains alone; but if it dies, it bears much fruit." (John 12:24)

Thus it would seem that the dying, the failure, the going down of the old is a necessary step in all true salvation. Every person must go down until he strikes his own level, his own self, before there can be any real growth. We may seem to hold another up for a while, but eventually he or she must walk alone. The time of walking alone with his or

her own indwelling Christ, his or her own true
self, will depend largely on our letting go of
him or her. No one will seek anything higher
than he is today, until the need of something
higher is felt. Your dear ones must have the
liberty to live out their own lives, and you
must let them, or else you are the one who
puts off the day of their salvation.

"But," says someone whose heart is aching
over the error ways of a loved one, "should
you not help anyone? Should you not run
after him, and urge him continually to turn
into the right way?"

Yes and no. I gladly, joyfully help anyone
when he or she wants help, but I could not
urge others to leave their own light and walk
by my light. Nor would I, like an overly fond
mother, pick up another and try to carry that
person in my arms by continually "treating"
him.

A mother may—and sometimes does, mentally and morally, if not physically—through
her false conception of love, carry her child
until he is twenty years old, lest he, not knowing how to walk, fall and bump his nose a few
times. But if she does this until he is grown,
what will he do? He will turn and rend her,
because she has stolen from him his inherent

right to become strong and self-reliant. She has interposed herself between him and the power within him that was waiting, from birth, to be his strength and sufficiency in all things. She should have placed him on his own feet, made him know that there was something in him that could stand, encouraged and steadied him, and so helped him to be self-reliant and independent.

Hundreds of anxious fathers and mothers, sisters and wives say, "Ah, but I love this one so I cannot stand still and see him rushing on to inevitable suffering."

Yes, you love this person. But it takes an infinitely greater, more Godlike love to stand still and see your child burn his hand a little, that he may gain self-knowledge, than it does to be a slave to him, ever on the alert to prevent the possibility of his learning through a little suffering. Are you equal to this larger love? Having come to a knowledge of the mighty truth that "God is all and in all," have you the moral courage to "be still, and know"; to take off all restrictions and rules from others, and to let the God within them grow them as He will; and, trusting Him to do it in the right way, keep yourself from all anxiety in the matter?

When Jesus preached of a glorious freedom from suffering, through a *"kingdom ... within,"* He often interspersed His preaching with the words: *"He who has ears to hear, let him hear."* (Mark 4:9) In other words, the Gospel message of deliverance is for all who are ready for it. Let him who has come to where he wants it, take it.

No one has a right to coerce another to accept his ideal. Every person has a right to keep his own ideal until he desires to change it.

God is leading your friend by a way you do not and cannot know. It is a safe and sure way; it is the shortest and only way. It is the Christ Way; the within way. "I am the door," says the Christ within every soul. *"If any man enter in,* (that is, by way of the Christ in himself) *he shall be saved."*

Now you are trying to have your friend enter through your door. Your friend must enter through his own Christ, his own desire, and you must leave him alone to the workings of that indwelling One if you want him to manifest good.

"But," you say, "is there nothing I can do when I see my friend going down?"

Yes, there is something you can do, and a

very effectual something too.

The sword of the Spirit . . . is the word of God. (Eph. 6:17) You can, whenever you think of your friend, speak the word of freedom to him or her. You can always and in all ways "loose him, and let him go," not forgetting that the letting go is as important as the loosing. Tell him mentally that Christ lives within him and makes him free, forever free; that he manifests the Holy One wherever he goes and at all times, for there is nothing else to manifest. Then see that you do not recognize any other manifestation than the good in him.

It is written: *"If you forgive the sins of any, they are forgiven; if you retain the sins of any, they are retained."* (John 20:23) Will you invariably speak the word of remission or loosing to your erring ones? Or will you bind them closer, tighter in the bondage that is breaking your own heart, by speaking the word of retention to them continually?

If you really want your friends to be free, loose them and let them go. For it is the promise of the Father, that: *". . . whatever you loose on earth shall be loosed in heaven."* (Matt. 16:19)

All-Sufficiency in All Things

There is that within every human being which is capable of being brought forth into the material, everyday life of any person as the abundance of every good thing that he may desire.

Here and there a person who is consciously abiding in the secret place of the Most High, and being taught by the Spirit of truth, dimly recognizes this, and says, "The Holy Spirit abiding within us is able to do all things for us"; while occasionally a metaphysician, in whom the intuitional is largely developed, is beginning to apprehend it as demonstrable Truth, and, carefully avoiding all pious words, lest he be considered in the old rut of

51

religious belief, says, "The outer or visible man has no need that the inner or invisible man cannot supply."

Let us not haggle over terms. There need be no schism. Each means the same thing. The only difference is in words. Each one is getting at the same Truth in his own way, and eventually the two will clasp hands in unity and see eye to eye.

The Spirit of the living God within us, fed ever from the Fountainhead, is not only the giver of all good gifts, the supplier of all supply, but is the gift itself. We must come right up to this point. The giver and the gift are one.

God Himself is the fulfillment—or the substance which fills full—of every desire.

Truly we are coming to know of "God in His world"; of God, the immanent creative Cause of all things, ever dwelling in us, ready and willing at any moment to re-create or renew our bodies and minds, or to manifest Himself through us as anything needed by us.

The certainty of this manifestation depends on the ability to recognize and accept Truth.

One recognizes God within as indwelling

purity and holiness. To this one God is sanctification, and in proportion to the recognition and the trust with which this divine presence is regarded as immanent holiness, does it spring forth into the outer, everyday life of a person as holiness, so that even they who run may perceive something more than human in him.

Another recognizes and accepts the God within himself as the life of his body, and instantly this divine life, always perfect, strong, and vigorous, and always desiring with the mighty desire of omnipotent love to manifest itself through someone or something as perfection, begins to flow through his body from center to circumference until his entire body is charged with a fullness of life that is felt even by others who come in contact with him. This is divine healing, and the time required for the process of complete healing depends, not on any changeableness of God—for God knows no time but the eternal now—but entirely on the ability of the person to recognize and trust the power that works in him.

The one who recognizes the indwelling God as his holiness, but cannot mentally grasp any more Truth, lives a holy, beautiful life, but perhaps lives it through years of bodily disease and sickness. Another who recognizes the same immanent God as his health, and is made both holy and physically well by the recognition and acceptance, stops there, and wonders, when he is well and living a life entirely unselfish and Godlike, why he should always be poor, lacking even the bare necessities of life.

Can you not see that this same indwelling God who is your holiness and your health is also your sustenance and support? Is God not our All-Sufficiency in all things? Is it not the natural impulse of the divine Being to flow forth through us into all things—*"whatever you ask in prayer..."*? (Matt. 21:22) Is there any limit, except as our poor human mind has set? He did say: *"Every place that the sole of your foot will tread upon I have given to you...."* (Josh. 1:3) What does this mean?

This divine energy is the substance (from *sub*, under, and *stare*, to stand), the real thing that stands under or within the visible or unreal of all things—food and clothing as well as life and health.

How do we get holiness? Not by outside works of purifying ourselves, but by turning to the Holy Spirit within and letting it flow forth into our human nature until we become permeated with the Divine. How is perfect health through divine or spiritual healing obtained? Is it by looking to or trusting external efforts or appliances? Surely not; but rather by ceasing entirely to look to the without, and turning our thoughts and our faith to the Father in us.

How, then, are we to get our abundant supply—even more than we can ask or think (for God gives not according to our need, but "according to his riches" we are told)?

Acquaint now thyself with him, and be at peace: thereby good shall come unto thee. . . . If thou return to the Almighty, thou shalt be built up . . . the Almighty shall be thy defence, and thou shalt have plenty of silver. (Job 22:21, 23, 25, A.V.)

It is not enough to believe simply that God is our supplier—the One who shall by His omnipotent power influence the mind of someone possessing an abundance to divide with us. This is limitation. God's being our health means far more than God's being our healer. God as our supply is infinitely more than God as our supplier. God is the Giver and the gift.

When Elisha multiplied the widow's oil, he did not, recognizing God simply as the supplier, ask, and then for answer receive a few barrels of oil from someone overly wealthy in that commodity, someone in whose heart the Spirit of God was working. That would have been a good but a very limited way, for had the demand continued, in time not only the village but the whole country around would have been destitute of oil.

Elisha understood the divine law of working, and put himself into harmony with it; then God Himself, the substance of all things, became manifest as the unlimited supply—a supply which could easily have flowed until this time had there been need and vessels enough.

Jesus' increase of the loaves and fishes did not come up from the village in response to some silent word spoken by Him to a person having a quantity. He never recognized that He had any right to seek the surplus possessions of another, even though He was going to use them to benefit others. In order to feed the multitude, He did not reach out after that which belonged to anyone, or even that which was already in manifestation. The extra supply was a new and increased manifestation of divine substance as bread and fish. So with the oil of Elisha, who was a man: "... *of like nature with you* ...." (Acts 14:15) In both these cases, nothing came from without to supply the need, but the supply proceeded from within outward.

This divine Substance—call it God, creative energy, or whatever you will—is ever abiding within us, and stands ready today to manifest itself in whatever form you and I need or wish to manifest, just as it did in Elisha's time. It is the same yesterday, today, and forever. Our desire is the cup that shapes the form of its coming, and our trust—the highest form of faith—sets the time and the degree.

Abundant supply by the manifestation of the Father in us, from within outward, is as much a legitimate outcome of the Christ life or spiritual understanding as is bodily healing.

The Word—or Spirit—is made flesh (or clothed with materiality) in both cases, and both are equally in God's order. The law of "work-to-earn" is only a schoolmaster beating us with many stripes, breaking us into many pieces when we fall across it in our failures, just to bring us to Christ. "But now that faith is come, we are no longer under a tutor." Then Christ—the Divine in us—becomes the fulfillment of the law.

"Do not labor for the food which perishes..." said the Nazarene. (John 6:27) Cease to work with the one object, namely, for a living or for supply. Be forever free from the law of poverty and want, as you are from the law of sin and disease—through faith in Christ; that is, by taking the indwelling Christ, or Spirit, or invisible man as your abundant supply, and, looking up to no other source, hold to it until it manifests itself as such. Recognize it. Reckon it. Be still and know it. Do not struggle and work and worry while you know it, but just be still. In Psalms 46:10 it says: *"Be still, and know that I am"*—what? Part of God? No. *"Know that I am God"*—all of God, all of good. I am life. I am health. I am love. I am supply. I am the substance of all that human souls and bodies can need or want.

The law says: *"In the sweat of your face you shall eat bread...."* (Gen. 3:19) The gospel brings: *"... good news of a great joy which will come to all the people...."* (Luke 2:10) The law says: work out your salvation from sin, sickness, and poverty. The gospel teaches that Christ, the Father in you, is your salvation. Have faith in Him. The law says: work all you can, and God will do the rest. The law is a way; Gospel, or Christ, is the Way: "... *choose this day whom you will serve* . . . ." (Josh. 24:15)

"But," says someone, "will not such teaching that our abundance is not at all dependent on the labor of our hands or head foster selfishness and indolence? Is it not a teaching dangerous to the masses?"

Jesus never thought the gospel dangerous for the masses. It has not proved dangerous to teach that health is a free gift of God—a gift that we need not labor for, but just recognize and accept.

Does anyone attempt to hide away from others, like a talent hidden deep in the earth, the newborn health that is God-manifest in response to recognition and faith? If he does, he soon finds that his health has disappeared, for selfishness and the consciousness of an indwelling God cannot both abide in the same heart.

Let not anyone for a moment suppose that he can use gospel means for selfish ends. The person may well suppose he can go west by going east. The divine abundance manifested through you is given you for ministry to others. You can neither receive it indolently nor retain it selfishly. If you attempt either, the flow of divine oil will be stopped.

In Christ, or in the consciousness of the indwelling divine Spirit, we know that every man and woman is our father and mother, brother and sister; that nothing is our own, but all is God's because all is God.

And because we know this, we give as we work without thought or hope of return, because God flows through us to others. Giving is our only safety valve. Abundance is often a snare to those who know not God, the indwelling One, who is love. But the abundance that is manifested from within outward is only the material clothing of perfect love, and cannot bring selfishness. *The blessing of the Lord makes rich, and he adds no sorrow with it.* (Prov. 10:22)

Will God, being manifest as our abundant supply, foster idleness? A thousand times, no! We shall then, more than ever, be coworkers with God, working but not laboring, working always for others. Work is labor only when it is for self. Labor, not work, brings weariness, sorrow, and sickness. Labor not for any good to yourself. Working as God works does not weary, for then the current of unlimited divine life is always flowing through us anew to bless others.

There is a river whose streams make glad ... (Psalms 46:4) but we must always keep the stream flowing from within—the source of its uprising—outward if it is to make glad. When we work in harmony with divine law, we have with us the whole force of the stream of living waters to carry us along.

Better than he knew, spoke the poet when he said: *Earth has no sorrow that heaven cannot heal.*

Not the faraway heaven after death, when a whole lifetime has been spent in sorrow and trouble, but the kingdom of heaven is here, now, today. The mortal, human, earth part of you has no sorrow that cannot be healed, overcome, wiped out at once and forever by this ever-indwelling divine Spirit.

If anyone would hasten the day of everyone's deliverance from all forms of human sorrow and want, let that person at once begin to withdraw himself from outside sources and external warfare, and center his thoughts on Christ the Lord within.

"Great in your midst is the Holy One...."
(Isa. 12:6)

Acquaint now thyself with him, and be at peace: thereby good shall come unto thee. (Job 22:21, A.V.)

Prove me now ... if I will not ... pour you out a blessing, that there shall not be room enough to receive it. (Mal. 3:10, A.V.)

Let us prove Him. ... *Commune with your own hearts on your beds; and be silent.* (Psalms 4:4) Be still and know. Be still and trust. Be still and expect.

For God alone my soul waits in silence, for my hope is from him. (Psalms 62:5)

God's Hand

There is but one hand in the universe. It is God's hand. Whenever you have felt that your hand was empty, it has been because you have believed yourself separate from God. Have you at times felt a great desire to give to others something they needed or wanted, yet have not been able to give? Have you said many times within yourself, "Oh, if I only had money, how I would relieve anxiety and distress! If it were only in my power, how quickly I would give a lucrative position to this one needing work, freedom to that one wanting release from material bondage," and so forth? Have you often said, "If I could only afford it, I would gladly give my time and service to others with no thought of return"?

From where, do you suppose, comes this desire to give? Is it from the mortal of you? No, it is the voice of the Giver of all good gifts crying out through you. It is God's desire to give through you. Cannot God afford to give whenever and wherever God will, and not be made poorer, but richer, thereby? Your hand is God's hand. My hand is God's hand. Our Father reaches out through these, His only hands, to give His gifts. We have nothing to do with the supply. Our part is to pass out the good gift, freely and without ceasing. This we can do only by making a complete consecration (so far as our consciousness goes) of our hands, our entire being, to the service of God, the All-Good. When we have given anything to others we no longer consider it our own, but recognize it as belonging to them. So this conscious consecration of our hands to God helps us to recognize them as God's hands in which is (no longer "shall be") the fullness of all things.

When first the full recognition of there being but one hand was given to a certain woman, it was so real that for hours whenever she looked at her right hand she seemed unable to close it, so full of all good things did it seem. She said to herself: "Then if this be true, I have, in my hand, health to give the sick, joy to give the mourning, freedom to give those in bondage, money to give those needing it; it only needs that I keep the hand open for all good gifts to flow out." To all who came to her that day in need of anything she said mentally: "Here is just what you desire; take it and rejoice. All my gifts are in my hand to give; it is God's hand."

And the result of that day's work almost startled her, with such marvelous swiftness did the external manifestations of the heart's desire come to everyone to whom she gave the word. One aged man, who for five years had been in external bondage and exile in a foreign land, held there by the machinations of another, and in which case no external law had been of avail to free, was set into perfect liberty, with the most complete vindication of character and consequent public congratulations and rejoicings, by the word of liberty spoken for him through this woman that day. Recognizing her hand as God's hand, she only said, "Then in this hand are that man's freedom papers," and mentally extending to him her hand she said, "Here is your freedom.

It is God's gift; wake up and take it; get up and go forth; you are free." Then she committed the whole matter to Him who invariably establishes the word spoken in faith, and He brought to pass the physical outpicturing of freedom.

Thou openest thy hand, thou satisfiest the desire of every living thing. (Psalms 145:16) Would you like to be able to do this? Then keep the hand open. Refuse to be hindered by fear of poverty, fear of want, fear that you will not be appreciated or justly dealt with. Go right on giving aid to all who need anything. "Only say the word" of giving. It is God's word spoken through your lips, and has He not said: "... *my word ... shall not return to me empty, but it shall accomplish that which I purpose ....*" (Isa. 55:11)

We cannot afford to withhold from giving our time, our intellect, our love, our money, to those who need, for the law is that withholding makes poorer. *There is that scattereth, and yet increaseth; and there is that withholdeth more than is meet, but it tendeth to poverty,* said Solomon. (Prov. 11:24, A.V.)

The supply is inexhaustible. Its outflow can be limited only by demand. Nothing can hinder the hand that is consciously recognized as God's hand from being refilled, except, as was the case when the widow's oil was multiplied through Elisha: ... *There is not a vessel more....* (II Kings 4:6, A.V.) Let not the seeming emptiness of your hand at times stagger your faith for a moment. It is just as full when you do not see it as when you do. Keep right on recognizing it as God's right hand in which are all good gifts now; thus you will prove Him who said: ... *prove me now herewith, saith the Lord of hosts, if I will not open you the windows of heaven, and pour you out a blessing, that there shall not be room enough to receive it.* (Mal. 3:10, A.V.)

God is surely calling us to "come up higher." To all those who are earnestly seeking Truth for Truth's sake, and not for the loaves and fishes, nor that they may be able to "give a sign" to those seeking signs, He is saying loudly: *"Therefore do not be anxious, saying, 'What shall we eat?' or 'What shall we drink?' or 'What shall we wear?'... your heavenly Father knows that you need them all. But seek first his kingdom and his righteousness, and all these things shall be yours as well."* (Matt. 6:31-33)

Freely ye have received, freely give. (Matt. 10:8, A.V.) *"... Love your enemies, and do good, and lend, expecting nothing in return; and your reward will be great, and you will be sons of the Most High . . . .* " (Luke 6:35) God is forever giving, giving, giving, with no thought of return. Love always thinks of giving, never of receiving. God's giving is the spontaneous outflow of perfect love. The higher we rise in recognition and consequent manifestation of the Divine, the more surely we think always of the giving, not of what we shall receive.

We know now that money, houses, lands, and all material things can be made to come to us by our holding them in our thoughts as ours, but that is not the highest that God has in store for us. *"What no eye has seen, nor ear heard, nor the heart of man conceived, what God has prepared for those who love him."* (I Cor. 2:9) What? Self? No, but "that love him"—that love good more than self. Jesus said: *". . . every one who has left houses . . . for my name's sake, will receive a hundred-fold . . . .* " (Matt. 19:29) They that have forsaken, they that have forsaken self, they that dare let their hands be forever open to their brothers, doing good and lending, hoping for nothing again, to them is the promise of a hundredfold even in this life.

God has called us to be His stewards. He has chosen us as vessels to carry good to others, and it is only while carrying to others that we can be filled. The law is: *"give, and it will be given to you; good measure, pressed down, shaken together, running over, will be put into your lap."* (Luke 6:38) Give without thought of return.

"But," says one, "am I to give my time, my money, my best thoughts to others and not require of them something in return? It is not just." Give as God gives. He knows no mine and yours. He says: "All things that are mine are yours."

Look only to God for supply. If anything is returned to you through the one to whom you give, render thanks for it. If nothing visible is returned, give thanks just the same, knowing that no man can stand between you and the inexhaustible supply; that it is he that withholds who is impoverished thereby, not he from whom anything is withheld.

"Agree with God, and be at peace; thereby good will come to you. . . . If you return to the Almighty and humble yourself, if you remove unrighteousness far from your tents, if you lay gold in the dust, and gold of Ophir among the stones of the torrent bed, and if the

Almighty is your gold, and your precious silver; then you will delight yourself in the Almighty, and lift up your face to God." (Job 22:21-26)

When we have learned that God is our supply, and that from Him comes all our help, we shall no longer care whether or not "pay" is rendered for our services. We shall simply know that all things are ours now, and out of the fullness of love we shall give freely. God's hand is sure. Your hand is God's hand now, today. It is full now. Give out of it mentally to all who call on you, whatever they need.

If Thou Knewest

It would seem almost childish, almost an insult to the intelligence of one's readers, to assert that the sunlight coming into a darkened room will annihilate the darkness. The merest child knows this, even if he does not understand the *modus operandi* of such fact. The sunlight does not have to make an effort to do this; it does not have to combat the darkness or wrestle or strain to overcome it; in fact, it does not change its course or its natural action in the least. It just goes on calmly radiating itself as usual. And yet the darkness is annihilated the instant it is touched by the light. Why? Because the darkness is not an entity having a reality of its own. It is no thing. It is simply the absence of a positive, real something. When there is made a way for the something to rush in and fill to fullness the empty space, the no thing then is the nothing, the darkness annihilated, destroyed, healed; all there is left is the something, the light.

Where did the darkness go? It did not go anywhere because it was not; it had not existed. It was simply the lack of something, and when the lack was filled there was no longer any lack. So it is with all negation, with all that is not good, not light, not love, not health, not wholeness. They are each and every one the absence of the real, and they are all annihilated or healed by letting in a something, a real substance that fills the vacuum.

Remembering that the things that are seen are the temporal and the unreal, which pass away, while the things that are not seen are the eternal, the real, let us carry this thought of the "no thing" a little further. Unhappiness is not a reality because it is not eternal; it belongs in the category of things that pass away. Envy, selfishness, jealousy, fear, and so forth are not real entities in our lives. Each is a lack of love, its positive opposite. Lack of temporal goods, lack of health, lack of wisdom—these things do not belong to the kingdom of the real because they are all temporal things that will, as the philosopher Epictetus said, pass away. Nothing is real except the eternal, that which is based on the real substance—God—that which can never be changed or made less by any external circumstances whatever.

Does this not make a little clearer and more acceptable, a little less antagonistic, the oft-repeated statements, "There is no evil; sickness is not real; sin is not real," and so forth? I repeat, nothing is real that is not eternal, and all conditions of apparent evil, of sickness, poverty, fear, and so forth, are not things, not entities in themselves, but they are simply an absence of the opposite good, just as darkness is the absence of light. In the deepest reality there is never an absence of the good anywhere, for that would mean absence of God. God as life, wisdom, love, substance, fills every place and space of the universe, or else God is not omnipresent. Who shall dare say God is not? Eventually our best healing of wrong conditions and human suffering is done when we recognize and affirm this great whole of Truth, the omnipresence of God, refusing absolutely to recognize anything else. The only "absence" that exists is in our consciousness or lower senses. But in order to bring this matter to the human understanding piecemeal, to break the bread so that each shall have the portion which he is able with his present growth to take, let us take up a little detail.

Your friend is to all appearances very ill. God is life—all the life there is in the universe. Is your friend's illness an entity, a "real" thing (that is, an eternal thing)? No, it is rather like the darkened room, needing only the light to heal, an absence of perfect life in the body. Would not the incoming of newness of life—this perfect life—to all the diseased atoms heal and renew and make alive? Of course. Well, how are we to let in this fullness of life? We shall see later.

Take another example, for bodily illness is one of the least of the woes of blinded humanity with which we have to deal. A mother's precious son is going all wrong. He drinks, steals; he breaks his mother's heart with his unkindness and his dissipation. She weeps, rebukes, entreats, lectures, finally nags. What is all this that is killing the mother? It is no thing, nothing at all. It is not real because it is not eternal. It is the absence of love, that is all. A perfect flood of love permeating and saturating that boy's being would heal all his diseases, both moral and physical, because he is simply manifesting a great selfishness that is absence of love—the darkened room again. How are we to get the remedy, fullness of love, let in and thus applied to the root of the disease? We shall see.

Poverty belongs among the no things, the nothings. It is not real, for only the eternal things are real, and poverty is temporal. It is an absence of substance and it is only permanently healed by an inflow of substance to fill the empty space. Sin is not real, for it is not eternal. It is failure to reach the mark. It is a blind, ignorant outreaching of the human for something possessed, the sinner desiring and hoping thereby to gain happiness. This empty void, this awful outreaching that resulted in failure, is only satisfied and healed by the incoming flood of good that fills the lack, as the sunlight fills the darkness.

In overcoming undesirable conditions in our life there are two ways of arriving in our consciousness at the realization of the omnipresence of God—the great, comprehensive

Truth, which heals all manner of diseases and which makes free. First, we persistently deny the reality of all seeming evil; second, we let in the substance of all good.

Everything undesirable passes away if we refuse to give it recognition by word, deed, or thought as a reality. This we can do more easily when we remember that nothing is real except the eternal. Paul said: ... *give no opportunity to the devil* (evil). (Eph. 4:27) It has no existence whatever, any more than has the darkness that often causes us fear and suffering. It has no more reality (remembering what is real) than the fiction of dreams. When one awakens from an unpleasant dream, some moments of assertion to oneself that it was only a dream, not real, are required before the heart's normal action returns and the natural breathing is restored. Even with one's eyes wide open, the dream seems strangely real, but we all know that it was a delusion of the senses, nothing else; it has no substance, no reality. So the physical and material troubles are not real, and they will disappear if we refuse to give them any life or reality by our word or thought. Let us rejoice in words of thanksgiving that this is one of God's ways, simply that evils are not.

This is our first step.

Now for the second step. Had a person any true conception of the gift of God to him, nothing in the created world would be able to withstand his power. We speak of a person's "gift" without realizing how truly we are speaking. We say he is gifted in this way or that, as though he were in possession by nature of some remarkable ability inherited from parents, or created by peculiar environment. While many of us are ready to acknowledge in a general way that: *Every good endowment and every perfect gift is from above, coming down from the Father of lights...* (James 1:17) even we are not prepared for the reception of the marvelous truth of endowment from the Source. When a glimpse of it comes, it makes one almost breathless with wonder and astonishment.

If thou knewest the gift of God.... (John 4:10, A.V.) What is this inestimable gift? What, indeed, but that He has given the veritable Son of God to be forever within us. This is the marvelous way of creation and also of redemption from all human lack and suffering, Christ-in-you. *For in him* (in this Christ, this Son of God) *the whole fullness of deity dwells bodily, and you have come to fulness of life in him* . . . (Col. 2:9, 10)—fullness of life, love, wisdom, substance yes, of the very substance of everything this human can need or desire. We can truly know that: *Christ, in whom are hid all the treasures of wisdom and hidden knowledge. . . .* (Col. 2:2, 3) . . . *From his fulness we have all received. . . .* (John 1:16)

To have created man thus seemed wise to infinite wisdom, and the one object in this life should be with us as it must be in the Mind of God, to make manifest this son of God. . . . *Grace was given* (power, love, life, wisdom, substance) *to each of us according to the measure of Christ's gift.* (Eph. 4:7) Not that God's giving is with partiality. Make no mistake here. The Creator of the universe is no respecter of persons. There are no favorites in God's creation. All the "fulness of deity" is embodied in His Son, this indwelling Christ. But this power, life, wisdom, this "all" that makes up the "fulness of deity," is manifested only in proportion as we recognize this Christ as the Source of the good that we desire, look to Him for it, acknowledge Him as All, and affirm persistently in the face of all opposition that the Son of God is now made visible through us.

Each of us is small or great, gifted or otherwise: ... *according to the measure of Christ's gift* (Eph. 4:7) we receive consciously. There must be an incoming of this divine Son of God to our conscious mind. The incoming will depend on our faithfulness in acknowledging the Source and affirming its manifestation. We cannot idly drift into it. We must speak the words of Truth before Truth will become manifest. John said: ... *The reason the Son of God appeared was to destroy the works of the devil* (evil). (I John 3:8) Precisely so, just as the light is manifested to destroy the darkness by filling it full. Let us take and definitely use, day after day, this statement of Truth: *The Son of God in me is now manifested, made visible in my body and all my affairs. He comes not to destroy, but to fill full.*

Trusting and Resting

There is a perfect passivity that is not indolence. It is a living stillness born of trust. Quiet tension is not trust. It is simply compressed anxiety.

Who is there among those who have learned the law of good and have tried to bring it into manifestation, who has not at times felt his or her physical being almost ready to snap with the intensity of "holding to the Truth." You believe in omnipresent life. You attempt to realize it for others. Someone comes to you for help, one who is always in a hurry for results, always wanting to know how much more time will be required, and so forth. The person's impatience and unbelief, together with your great desire to prove the law to him, stimulate you, after a few treatments, to greater efforts; and almost immediately you find yourself thinking frequently of the person when not treating, and trying to throw more force into the treatment when the person is present.

Then, after giving a treatment, you find a sense of fullness in your head that is very uncomfortable; and very soon, what at first was a delight to you becomes a burden, and you almost wish the patient would go to someone else. You cannot help wondering why the person improved so perceptibly with the first few treatments, and afterward, even with your increased zeal, seemed to stand still and get worse. Let me tell you why. When you first began to treat, you, so sure of the abundance of divine life, calmly and trustingly spoke the Truth to your patient. When the person got in a hurry, you, beginning to take on responsibility that was God's, not yours, grew anxious and began to cast on him your compressed anxiety. You were no longer a channel for divine life, sweet, peaceful, harmonious, to flow through, but by your intensity and hurry, you completely shut off the divine influx and were able only to force on the person, out of your anxious mortal mind, a few strained, compulsory thoughts that held him as in a vise, and exhausted you.

Some healing and other demonstrations of power are brought to pass in this way, but it is always the stronger mortal thought controlling the weaker, and is always wearing to the one thus working. This plane is entirely one of mental suggestion, a mild form of hypnotism.

In the matter of God as our supply, or any other side of the divine law that we, from time to time, attempt to bring into manifestation, the moment we begin to be anxious, our quiet becomes simply the airtight valve of tension or suppressed anxiety that shuts out the very thing we are trying to bring about, and so prevents its manifestation.

This way of holding with intensity to a thought, be it mental argument for healing or looking to God for material supply, recognizing that we have power by such firmness of thought to bring what we want into manifestation, is one way of obtaining results, but it is a hard way. We therefore give out what is within us, and it is helpful so far as it goes, but by some mental law this intensity of thought seems to cut off our consciousness

from the Fountainhead, thus preventing inflow and renewal from God, resulting in the
quick exhaustion and the burdened feeling.

We need to rise above this state of tension
to one of living trust. There is such a thing as
an indolent shifting of our responsibility to
an outside God, which means laziness, and
which never brings anything into manifestation. But there is also a state of trustful
passivity, into which we must enter to do the
highest work.

There are some things that we are to do
ourselves, but there are others that God does
not expect us to do. (When I speak of ourselves as something apart from God, I simply
mean our conscious selves. We are always one
with God, but we do not always consciously
realize it. I speak of ourselves as the
conscious part of us.) They are His part, and
our greatest trouble lies in our trying to do
God's part, just because we have not learned
how to trust God to do it. We are, with our
conscious thought, to speak the words of life,
of Truth, of abundant supply, and we are to
act as though the words were true. But the
"bringing it to pass" is the work of a power
that is higher than we; a Presence that we do
not see with these mortal eyes, but which is

omnipotent and will always rush to our rescue when we trust it.

From the smallest thing of our everyday life to the rolling away of the largest stone of difficulty from our path, this Presence will deliver us. But its working depends on our trusting, and trusting means getting still inside.

In our effort to bring into manifestation the good that we know belongs to every child of God, it is when we get beyond the point where we try to do it all ourselves and let God do His part that we get the desires of our heart.

After we have done our part faithfully, earnestly, we are told to: ... *stand still, and see the salvation of the Lord, which he will shew to you today . . . . The Lord shall fight for you, and ye shall hold your peace.* (Exod. 14:13, 14, A.V.) See the conditions here imposed. This invisible Presence will remove from your path the difficulties, which look to your mortal vision to be almost insurmountable, only if you stand still. The Lord will fight for you if you hold your peace. But there is no promise of deliverance for you while you preserve a state of unrest within. Either a state of internal unrest, or a forced external quiet, which simply means compressed anxiety, prevents this invisible omnipotent force from doing anything for your deliverance. It must be peace, peace; possess your soul in peace, and let God work.

Marvelous have been the manifestations of this power in my life when the "bringing to pass" has been left entirely to it. Ask not, then, when or how or why. This implies doubt. *Be still before the Lord, and wait patiently for him . . . .* (Psalms 37:7)

When, in the reign of Jehoshaphat, King of Judah, the Ammonites, Moabites, and others —a great multitude—came against the King in battle, he, in great fear, called the people together, and they sought counsel of the Lord, saying: "*. . . we are powerless against this great multitude that is coming against us. We do not know what to do, but our eyes are upon thee.*" (II Chron. 20:12) Then the Spirit of the Lord came upon Jahaziel, and he said: "*Hearken, all Judah . . . Thus says the Lord to you, 'Fear not, and be not dismayed at this great multitude; for the battle is not yours but God's. . . . You will not need to fight in this battle; take your position, stand still, and see the victory of the Lord on your behalf' . . . tomorrow go out against them,* *and the Lord will be with you.*" (II Chron. 20:15, 17)

My friend, the battle you are trying to fight is not yours, but God's. You are trying to heal; you are trying to hold vigorously to the law of good in that very trouble at home which the world knows not of, but which at times nearly overwhelms you. Be still. Let go. The battle is God's, not yours, and because it is God's battle through you, God desiring to manifest through you, victory was on your side before the battle began (in your consciousness, for that is the only place where there is any battle). Can you not calmly—even with rejoicing—claim the victory right now, because it is God's battle? You need no longer fight this battle, but "stand still," right where you are today, in the struggle to overcome material things, and "see the victory of the Lord on your behalf."

Does some doubting Thomas say, "Yes, but I must have money today," or "I must have relief at once or this salvation will come too late to be of use; and besides I do not see how"? Stop right there, dear friend. You do not have to see how. That is not your business. Your business is to "stand still" and proclaim, "It is done."

God said to Jehoshaphat: "... *Tomorrow go out against them ...* "; that is, they were to do calmly and in order the external things that were in the present moment to do, but at the same time they were to stand still or be in a state, mentally, of trustful passivity, and see God's saving power. Jehoshaphat did not say, "But, Lord, I do not see how"; or "Lord, I must have help right away or it will be too late, for already the enemy is on the road." We read: ... *they rose early in the morning ... and as they went out, Jehoshaphat stood and said, "Hear me, Judah. ... Believe in the Lord your God, and you will be established ...."* (II Chron. 20:20) And then he appointed singers, who should go forth before the army, singing: *"Give thanks to the Lord, for his steadfast love endures for ever."* (II Chron. 20:21)

All this, and not yet any visible sign of the promised salvation of the Lord! Right into the very face of battle against an army mighty in number, singing, "Give thanks to the Lord.

Are you any nearer than this to the verge of the precipice in this material condition that you are trying to overcome? What did Jehoshaphat do? Did he begin to think or pray hard and forcibly? Did he begin to send strong thoughts of defeat to the opposing army, and exhaust himself with his efforts to hold on to the thought until he should be delivered? Did he begin to doubt in his heart? Not at all. He simply remembered that the battle was God's and that he had nothing to do with the fighting, but everything to do with the trusting. Further on we read: *And when they began to sing and praise, the Lord set an ambush against the men of Ammon, Moab, and Mount Seir, who had come against Judah, so that they were routed.* (II Chron. 20:22)

It was only after they began to sing and to praise, that the Lord made the first visible move toward the manifestation of His promised salvation. It may be so with you. You may be at the very verge of apparent failure and the overthrow of the cherished principle. Your "friends" are already beginning to speak disparagingly to you of your foolish trust saying, "You must do something in this matter." Fear not. Just try to realize that the battle is God's through you; that because it is God's battle, it has been victory from the start and can never be anything else. Begin to sing and praise God for deliverance; and as surely as you do this, giving no thought to the when or the how, the salvation of the Lord will be made visible, and the deliverance as real as it was in Jehoshaphat's case, even to the gathering of unexpected "spoils" will follow. For this narrative of Judah's king further says:

When Judah came to the watchtower of the wilderness, they looked toward the multitude; and behold, they were dead bodies lying on the ground; none had escaped. When Jehoshaphat and his people came to take the spoil from them, they found cattle in great numbers, goods, clothing, and precious things, which they took for themselves until they could carry no more. They were three days in taking the spoil, it was so much. (II Chron. 20:24, 25)

So God delivers when fully trusted—perfectly, fully, even beyond anything we have asked or thought; adding good that we have never dreamed of, as though to give double assurance of God's favor and love to any who will trust God. This is the "victory of the Lord on your behalf" when you "stand still."

We must learn that the time of help's coming to us is not our part, but God's. We do know that in all the accounts in Scripture of those who realized God's special deliverance from their troubles—from Abraham's going forth to sacrifice his son, to the time when Jesus put out His hand to save the sinking and faithless Peter, and even after this in the experience of the apostles—this invisible power came to hand just at the right time always, never a moment too late.

The promise is: *God shall help her, and that right early* (Psalms 46:5, A.V.) or, as the Hebrew reads, "at the turning of the morning," which means the darkest moment before dawn. So if, in whatever matter you are trying to exercise trust in your Father, the way grows darker and the help goes farther away instead of coming into sight, you must grow more peaceful and still than ever, and then you may know that the moment of deliverance is growing nearer with your every breath.

In Mark's account of that early morning visit of the women to the tomb of Jesus, when bent on an errand of loving service, they forgot the immense stone lying across their path, until they were almost at their journey's end, and then one exclaimed in momentary dismay: *"Who will roll away the stone for us from the door of the tomb?"* And *looking up, they saw that the stone was rolled back—it was very large.* (Mark 16:3, 4) Is not "very large" full of meaning? The very greatness of the difficulty that made it impossible for the women to remove it was the more reason why it was done by this invisible Power.

"Man's extremity is God's opportunity." The more we are cut off from human help, the greater claim we can make on divine help. The more impossible a thing is to human or mortal power, the more at peace we can be when we look to the Lord for deliverance, for the Lord said: "*. . . my power is made perfect in weakness.*" (II Cor. 12:9) And Paul, realizing that when he placed less confidence in the mortal he had more help from the Divine, said: *. . . when I* (the mortal) *am weak, then I am strong.* (II Cor. 12:10)

Trusting means resting confidently. We are to rest confidently, saying: "God is my strength; God is my power; God is my assured victory. I will trust in Him, and He will bring it to pass."

Take delight in the Lord,
  and he will give you the desires of your
    heart.

(Psalms 37:4)

It is better to take refuge in the Lord
than to put confidence in princes.
                                   (Psalms 118:9)

Thou dost keep him in perfect peace,
whose mind is stayed on thee,
because he trusts in thee.
                                   (Isa. 26:3)

The Spoken Word

Without him (the Word) *was not anything made that was made.* (John 1:3)

In the beginning God created the heavens and the earth.

How?

Listen: *The earth was without form and void, and darkness was upon the face of the deep....*

And God said, "Let there be light"; and there was light....

And God said, "Let there be a firmament ...." And it was so.

And God said, "Let the waters under the heavens be gathered together into one place, and let the dry land appear." And it was so.

And God said, "Let the earth put forth vegetation...." And it was so.

Then, God said, "Let us make man in our image, after our likeness...." (Gen. 1:1-3, 6, 7, 9, 11, 26)

God, infinite power, might have thought about all these things till doomsday. He might have wished during an indefinite time that they were formed and made visible. Nothing would ever have been created in visible form had there not been the spoken word put forth into the formless ether. It took the definite positive "Let there be," to bring forth order out of chaos and to establish in visible results the thoughts and desires of even an infinite, omnipotent Creator.

To create is to bring into visibility; to form something where before there was nothing; to cause to exist or to take form that which before was without form and void. To exist (from *ex*, out from, and *sistere*, to stand) is to stand out. Being always is; existence (from Latin, *existere*, to stand forth, emerge, appear) is that which stands forth as a visible entity.

God creates. Because man was created or brought into the visible universe in the image and likeness of God, he, spiritually, has like powers with God: he has the power of creating, of bringing into visible form that which before did not exist. As God created by the spoken word, without which *was not anything made that was made,* so man can create by his spoken word. In fact, there is no other way to bring into existence the visible conditions and the things that we want.

Today scientists agree (material as well as spiritual) that there is but one universal substance out of which all things are made. This substance is divine stuff that, though invisible and intangible, is lying all about us, as is the atmosphere. This divine substance is without form and void, as is also this same physical atmosphere. It is waiting, forever waiting, for us to form it as we will, by our spoken word.

What is liquid air? It is compressed invisibility, is it not? It is invisible, formless substance pressed into form by a definite and continued process until it becomes visible and tangible. This God stuff, divine substance, is likewise subject to the pressure of our thought and word.

There are three realms in the universe: the spiritual, the mental or psychic, and the physical or material. These three, while in a way distinct, are so blended into one that it is difficult to know where one ends and another begins. All created things have Spirit, soul, and body. All things that we desire are now in being in the spiritual or invisible. But, as someone has said, thought and the spoken word stand between the invisible and the visible. By the action of these two—thought and the spoken word—is the invisible made visible.

When we desire anything—I use this word "anything" advisedly, for did not the Master say: "*. . . whatever you ask in prayer . . .*"? (Matt. 21:22) We must take our thought off the visible world and center it on God. We begin, as God began in creation, by speaking out into this formless substance all about us with faith and power, "Let there be so and so (whatever we want). Let it come forth into manifestation here and now. It does come forth by the power of my word. It is done; it is manifest." We continue this with vehemence a few moments and then let go of it. This should be repeated with firmness and regularity and definite persistence, at least in the morning and in the evening. Continue it, regardless of any evidence or want of evidence. Faith takes hold of the substance of the things hoped for and brings into evidence the things not seen.

The moment one takes cognizance of circumstances, that moment he lets go of faith.

Our spoken word first hammers the thing desired into shape. Our continued spoken word brings this shaped substance forth and clothes it with a visible body. The first action brings that which is desired from the formless toward the external as far as the psychic; the continued action brings it forth still farther and clothes it with visible form or material body.

This was illustrated to me a few years ago. A woman had been for days vigorously "speaking the word" for something she much desired. She had no confidante and recognized no human help.

One day she wrote an ordinary business letter to a friend in the country. This friend, on receipt of the letter, immediately replied, saying: *What is this strange thing about this letter of yours? When I took it from the post office it had the appearance to me of being covered with so and so* (the very thing which the writer had been shaping in the invisible by her spoken word). *I opened the letter,* she continued, *and for some minutes the opened letter took the form, to my sight, of a "horn of plenty," pouring out in unlimited quantity this same thing. Have I gone crazy, or what does it mean?*

The word spoken by the woman, alone in the silence of her own room, had shaped and brought forth toward the external, as far as the psychic realm, the thing desired. The vibrations of her thought had permeated, all unknown to her, everything that she had touched. The friend, having psychic power, saw, plainly surrounding this letter, the shape that the woman had created, though it was yet invisible to the natural eye. It is needless to say that the continued word very soon brought this shape forth into the visible world as a solid manifestation of exactly what the woman desired.

In this process, there are two things you must do. One is, do not talk with anyone about what you are doing. Talk scatters the precious divine substance. Needless talk diffuses and wastes one's power. It is impossible both to diffuse and to focus at the same time.

The other important thing you must do is continue with the spoken word.... *Let us not grow weary in well-doing, for in due season we shall reap, if we do not lose heart.* (Gal. 6:9)

Unadulterated Truth

There is a straight white line of absolute Truth upon which each one must walk to have demonstration. The slightest swerving in either direction from this line results in non-demonstration, no matter how earnest or intense one may be.

The line is this: *There is only God; all seeming else is a lie.*

Whoever is suffering today from sickness, poverty, failure—any kind of trouble—is believing otherwise.

We talk largely about Truth, and quote with ease and alacrity the words of the Master: "*... the Truth will make you free.*" (John 8:32) Free from what? Free from sickness, sorrow, weakness, fear, poverty. We claim to know the Truth, but the question is, are we free from these undesirable things? And if not, why not?

Let us be practical about this matter. We talk much about the omnipresence of God. In fact, this is one of the basic statements upon which rests New Thought. "God is omnipresent, omnipotent, omniscient." When I was a child in spiritual things, I thought as a child and understood as a child. I believed that God was here, there, and everywhere, within hailing distance of every human being, no matter whether under the sea or on the mountaintop, in prison or outside, in a hospital or at the wedding feast. In any and all places God was so near that in an instant God could be summoned to help. To me this was God's omnipresence. Then God's omnipotence meant to me that while sickness and poverty, sorrow, the evil tongue of jealousy or slander, and so forth, had great power to make one suffer, God had greater power. I believed that if God were called on to help us, God surely would do it, but it would be after a fierce and prolonged combat between the two powers of good and evil, or of God and trouble.

I wonder if there are others today whose

real, innermost thoughts of God's omnipresence and omnipotence are much like this. Are
you one of those who believe in God and
something else? God and sickness? God and
poverty? God and something unpleasant in
your life that you are daily trying to elimi-
nate by applying a sort of plaster of formal
statements of Truth over the sore place of
your trouble, while at the same time you are
giving in your own mind (if not also in your
conversation) almost equal power to the
remedy and the disease? While you remain in
this, you will never escape from your bondage, whatever it may be.

Try for a moment to think what is meant
by omnipresent Spirit, remembering at the
same time that what applies to your body
applies equally to all other forms of human
affairs or conditions.

Each little atom of one's physical body,
taken separately, is completely filled, permeated by Spirit life. This must be true
because there could be no external form to
the atom without first the *sub-stans*, that
which stands under, or as the basis of all
material things. The Spirit permeating each
atom is now, always has been, and always will
be absolutely perfect, because it is God, the

only life in the universe. These atoms are held together each moment by the same Spirit. They work together because the Spirit pervading them is one Spirit and not several spirits. Spirit life cannot change because if it did, there would be one place where, for a time, there would be lack of God, perfect life. One place for one instant without God would break up the entire law of omnipresence, which cannot be.

Jesus said: "*... the truth will make you free.*" (John 8:32) But He prefaced this statement by the words: "*... you will know the Truth....*" It is, then, knowledge of the Truth that sets free. We are free now but we do not know it. You may be the child of a king, but if you do not know it, you may live in poverty and squalor all your life. We are all, today, this very hour, free from all sickness, because God, who is perfect life, unchangeable and indestructible, abides within and completely fills every atom of our bodies. If God, divine substance, fills every part, every place and space, as the atmosphere fills the room, there is certainly no absence of Spirit life in any part. Then if today we are manifesting sickness, it is because we have believed the lie about ourselves and have reaped the results of the lie—that is, apparent lack of health—in our consciousness.

All that is, is good. But lack of God in any part is not; that is, does not exist. Such a thing is a mortal impossibility.

Many people are greatly puzzled by this. They are told that "there is no evil; all is good because all is God," and so forth. When they find themselves or others suffering pain, sickness, lack of money, and so forth, they are staggered in faith, and begin to say: "Surely this is not good; lack of health is not good; sin is not good; poverty is not good. What is this?" For an answer they are often told, "Oh, yes, this is good, for there is nothing but good (God) in the universe. This is unripe good, like the green apple."

Now the truth is that all which is not good (God) is no thing. It is the lie, and has only to be characterized as such in order to disappear. What is the wild beast that sits on your chest with such overwhelming weight when you have a nightmare? Is it "unripe good"? Is it something that, after a few days or weeks or right thoughts, you can manipulate into good? Not at all. From beginning to end it is nothing, no thing but a vagary, a deception of the mortal brain and senses. Had it at any time any sort of reality whatever? Surely not. It is all a lie, which, at the time, seems so real that it requires almost super-human efforts to throw it off, even after you realize that it is only a nightmare.

There is one God, the Father, from whom are all things . . . said Paul. (I Cor. 8:6) And again: *For from him and through him and to him are all things. . . .* (Rom. 11:36)

If God, then, is the substance of all things visible and invisible, and is omnipresent, there is no such thing as lack of God or lack of substance in any place in this universe. Sickness would be lack of life in some part of the body. Impossible! Poverty would be lack of substance in the circumstances. Impossible! Foolishness, ignorance, insanity, would be lack of God, Divine Mind, omniscience in man. Impossible! These things cannot be.

Do you not see, then, how all these negatives are nothingness, not true, the lie? And how, instead of recognizing them as something to be overcome, we should put them at once and at all times into their real place of nothingness?

Let us go back to our straight, white line of absolute Truth: *There is only God.* All that is not God is no thing, has no existence—is simply the nightmare. If we walk on this white line where we refuse to see or acknowledge anything but God, then all else disappears. In dealing with the everyday problems of life, we shall succeed in becoming free, in proportion as we cease to parley with apparent evils as though they were entities. We cannot afford to spend a moment's time agreeing with their claim, for if we do, we shall be the overcome instead of the overcomers. We must rise to the highest, most sweeping statements of Truth that we know. Our great statement must be: *"There is only God."* Whatever is not God (good) is a lie. And this lie must be instantly and constantly crushed on the head as a viper the moment it appears in our mentality. Hit the hydra-headed monster (the lie) as soon as it appears, with the positive statement, "You are a lie. Get to where you belong. There is no truth in you. There is only God, and God is fullness of good, life, joy, peace, now and forever."

The truth is there is no real lack anywhere, but a waiting abundance of every kind of good that we can possibly desire or conceive of. Stop believing the lie. Stop speaking it. Speak the Truth. It is the spoken Truth that makes manifest.

In the domain of Spirit there is neither time nor space. What is to be and already is must be spoken into visibility. Practice thinking and realizing omnipresence, that is, practice realizing that all good that you desire is here now, all-present; it is not apart from you and its coming to you does not require time. There is no time or space.

There is not God and—a body.

There is not God and—circumstance.

There is not God and—any sort of trouble.

There is only God through all things—in our bodies, in our seemingly empty purses, in our circumstances—just waiting as invisible Spirit substance for us to recognize and acknowledge Him, and Him only, in order to become visible. All else is a lie.

God is.

God is all.

God is manifest, because there is nothing else to manifest.

Oneness with God

Ralph Waldo Emerson said: *Prayer that craves a particular commodity, anything less than all good, is vicious. Prayer is the contemplation of the facts of life from the highest point of view. It is the soliloquy of a beholding and jubilant soul. It is the Spirit of God pronouncing His works good. But prayer as a means to effect a private end is meanness and theft. It supposes dualism and not unity in nature and consciousness. As soon as the man is [consciously] at one with God, he will not beg.*

True prayer then, is just a continual recognition and thanksgiving that all is good, and that all good is ours now as much as it ever can be. Oh, when will our faith become strong and steadfast enough to take possession of our inheritance here? The Israelites entered not into the Promised Land because of their unbelief. Their inheritance was real and was awaiting them then and there, but it could not do them any good nor give any enjoyment until they took hold of it by faith, after which and as a result of which, would have come the reality. It is this taking by faith that brings something into actuality and visibility.

Why do our mortal minds postpone the acceptance of all good as our rightful inheritance for this life? The heir of material wealth must accept his inheritance before he can possibly come into its possession or use. So long as he rejects it, he is as poor as though nothing had been provided for him. All things are ours now—fullness of love, of life, of wisdom, of power—even more than these, fullness of all good, which means abundance of all things, material as well as spiritual. *Every good endowment and every perfect gift is from above, coming down from the Father of lights with whom there is no variation or shadow due to change.* (James 1:17)

Many of God's children are ceasing to look at the things of God from the objective standpoint, and are learning to contemplate the facts of life from the subjective, or higher side—even pronouncing all things good, as God does, until everything else but the thought of good drops out of mind and only the good is manifest.

How marvelous are the little glimpses we from time to time obtain of things as God sees them! To what high points of privilege are we, God's children, being lifted so that it is possible for us to see things from the standpoint of pure intelligence, perfect wisdom! *"Truly, I say to you, many prophets and righteous men longed to see what you see, and did not see it . . . ."* (Matt. 13:17)

One instant's view of the facts of life from the subjective side (God's side) makes all our carnal aspirations and struggles, all our ambitions, all our boasted wisdom and pride sink into utter nothingness. We see instead *the wisdom of this world is folly with God.* (I Cor. 3:19) All other objects in life fade into insignificance beside the one of getting more into conscious oneness with the Father, where, at all times, we shall pray the true prayer of rejoicing and thanksgiving that all good is the only real thing in the universe. When we come into perfect recognition of unity instead of duality, then, indeed, shall we know prayer to be but the *soliloquy of a beholding and jubilant soul,* and we shall cease forever to pray the prayer as a means to effect a private end.

The nearer we approach to God, and the more we grow into the realization of our true relationship to Him, our Father, the more surely are all personalities, all divisions lost sight of; our oneness with all people becomes so vivid and real to us that a prayer for "private ends" becomes impossible to us. All desires of the little self are merged in the desire for universal good, because we recognize but One in the universe, and ourselves as part of that One.

How can we most quickly and surely attain this conscious oneness with the Father, which will enable us to see things as He sees them—all good?

Instantly flashes into the intuition, out from the stillness of the invisible, a voice saying, "Return to God." Return, turn away from the mortal, away from people, from human ways; turn *within* and look to God.

Seek the light from the interior, not from

external sources. Why always seek to inter-pose human help between ourselves and God? Emerson says: *The relations of the soul to the divine spirit are so pure that it is profane to seek to interpose helps. . . . Whenever a mind is simple and receives a divine wisdom, old things pass away—means, teachers, texts, temples fall.*

Let us not roam, let us stay home with the cause.

Constant reading, discussions, interchange of opinions are all external ways of reaching the Truth from the intellectual side. These are a way, but *"I am the way, and the truth, and the life . . ."* (John 14:6) said the voice of the Father through the Nazarene. . . . *The anointing which you received from him abides in you, and you have no need that any one shall teach you . . . .* (I John 2:27) *"When the Spirit of truth comes, he will guide you into all the truth . . . he will declare to you the things that are to come."* (John 16:13)

When will we cease running after Truth, and learn to *"be still, and know that I am God . . ."*? (Psalms 46:10)

In order that we may hear the inner voice and may receive the highest form of teaching, which alone can open the eyes of our spiritual understanding, the mortal self must cease its clamoring even for Truth; the human intellect must become absolutely still, forgetting to argue or discuss. The Father can lead into all Truth only when we listen to hear what He will say—not to what others will say. We must learn to listen—not anxiously and with strained ears, but expectantly, patiently, trustingly. We must learn how to wait on God, in the attitude of: " *'Speak, Lord, for thy servant hears'* " (I Sam. 3:9) if we would know Truth.

Jesus said: *". . . unless you turn and become like children* (that is, teachable and trusting), *you will never enter the kingdom of heaven"* (Matt. 18:3) or the kingdom of understanding of Truth. And again He said: *"I thank thee, Father . . . that thou hast hidden these things from the wise and understanding and revealed them to babes . . . ."* (Matt. 11:25)

We must put aside all preconceived opinions of Truth, either our own or any other person's, and with receptive minds opened toward the source of all light, say continually, "Lord, teach me." We must become as babes in human wisdom before we can enter into the deep things of God.

But believe me, the revelation that the Spirit of truth will make to you when you have withdrawn from all outside sources and learned to listen to the voice in your own soul, will be such as to make you know—no longer believe—your oneness with the Father and with all His children. They will be such as to fill you with great joy. *"These things I have spoken to you, that my joy may be in you, and that your joy may be full."* (John 15:11)

The great God of the universe has chosen you and me through whom to manifest. *"You did not choose me, but I chose you...."* (John 15:16) Shall we forever limit this manifestation by making ourselves into a little, narrow mold of personality that will shape and size the Divine, or worse still, shall we run here and there to borrow some measure our neighbor has made of himself, and hold it as our measure under the great rushing waters of infinite wisdom and love, thereby saying: "This full is all I want; it is all there is to be had, all that thou art"?

Away forever with such limitations!

> *There's a wideness in God's mercy,*
> *Like the wideness of the sea:*
> *There's a kindness in His justice,*
> *Which is more than liberty.*

For the love of God is broader
Than the measure of man's mind;
And the heart of the Eternal
Is most wonderfully kind.
                    —Frederick W. Faber

Would you, then, know God, "whom to know aright is life eternal"? Go not abroad looking for the Divine. "Stay at home within thine own soul." Seek earnestly, calmly, trustfully, the source of all good. Know at once and forever that only therein will you find Truth, and only thereby will you grow to be what you desire—centered, poised. Let go your narrow thoughts of the Divine, cease to desire anything less than the fulfillment of God's will in you. God's thoughts are higher than ours as the heavens are higher than the earth. Let nothing short of the perfect fulfillment of God thought in and through you satisfy you.

Do you comprehend this in its fullness—the desire of infinite love and pure intelligence being fulfilled (or filled full) in you and me?

How quickly and far recede the cankering cares of life, the frets and fumes, the misunderstandings and the being misunderstood! How sure we are when we have

consciously—and by effort if need be—swept
away all limitations of personal desire and are
saying, "Here I am, infinite Father, great
Fountainhead of all good. I have no desire.
You are fulfilling Your highest thoughts in
me, unhindered by my consciousness; You
are now pouring Yourself through this
organism into visibility; You are thinking
Your thoughts through this intellect; You are
loving through this heart with Your own
tender Father-Mother love, which thinks no
evil, endures all things, bears all things, and
seeks not its own; You are manifesting Yourself in Your own way through this organism
into the visible world."

I say, when we thus burst the bonds of personal desire and rise to a willingness that the
Father's will be done through us every moment, how sure we are of the fatherly care
that will clothe us with the beauty of the lilies
and feed us as the birds of the air. Indeed,
with even a more lavish abundance of all good
things than He gives to either of these, for
". . . . *you are of more value than many spar-
rows.*" (Matt. 10:31)

Do you fear to break loose from teachers,
from human helps? Fear not. Trust to the
great and Mighty One that is in you and is

limitless to manifest as Truth to you and
through you. There will be no failure, no mistake. Spend some time daily alone with the
Creator. In no other way will you come into
the realization that you desire. Learn to sever
yourself from those around you. Practice
this, and soon you can be as much alone with
God in the street or in a crowded room as you
could be in the wilds of a desert. A little book
called, "The Practice of the Presence of God,"
by Brother Lawrence, tells how he, for years,
kept himself consciously in the glory of
divine Presence, even while at the most humble daily tasks, by keeping the thought: "I
am in His presence." All things that were not
divine in the man died out and dropped away,
not because he fought them or resisted the
uprising of the natural man, but because he
persistently practiced the Presence (or
thought of the Presence) of God, and in that
Presence all other things melted away like
snow before a spring sun.

This is the only way of growth of overcoming. *Have this mind among yourselves,
which is yours in Christ Jesus . . . .* (Phil. 2:5)
We do not have, by some supreme effort, to
draw this Mind into us, but simply to let it
come into us. Our part is to take the attitude

consciously of receiving, remembering first to enter the "inner chamber" of our own soul, and to shut the door on all thought but that of divine Presence.

Each individual has his own salvation to work out—that is, his own true self to bring into visibility. This is not to be done by some intense superhuman effort, but by each one dealing directly with the Father.

So long as anyone clings to another, just so long will the manifestation of the real self, God, remain weak and limited. Wait only on God for the light you desire. He will tell you how to act, what to do. Trust your own inspiration; act on it, though all the world sit in judgment on it, for when any man puts aside selfish aims, and desires only to manifest the Highest, his life then becomes the perfect One manifesting through him.

When you learn to let God manifest through you, it will not be like the manifestation through anyone else. You will think and speak and do without previous thought or plan. You will be as new and surprising to yourself as to anyone else. For it will not be you speaking, but the Spirit of your Father speaking in and through you.

Oh, what supreme tranquillity we have

when we are conscious that our thought is God's thought through us; our act, our word, God's act and word through us! We never stop to think of results; that is God's care. We are quietly indifferent to criticism of lesser minds (mortal thought), for we know whom we have believed. We know that what we speak and do is right, though all the world be made wrong thereby. *What I must do is all that concerns me, not what the people think,* says Emerson. Then God in you becomes a law to you, and you no longer have need of external laws. God becomes wisdom to you, ever revealing to you more of Himself, giving you new and clear visions of Truth, and indeed: . . . *you have no need that any one shall teach you* . . . . (I John 2:27) You no longer have use for external forms, which are but the limitations of Truth and not Truth itself. Then God shall be to you, and through you to others, not only wisdom and understanding, but love and life and the abundance of all things needful.

Then shall you have at all times something new to give to others, instead of looking to them to receive; for you will stand in the very storehouse of all good with the Master of the house, that through you the Master may pass out freely the bread and water of life to those who are still holding up their empty cups to some human hand to be filled—not yet having learned to enter into all the fullness of good.

Believe me, you who seek Truth, who seek life and health and satisfaction, it is nowhere to be found until you seek it directly from the Fountainhead who gives to all.

Begin at once to put aside all things that you have previously interposed between your own soul and the great cause of all things.

Cease now and forever to lean on anything less than the Eternal. Nothing less can give you peace.

Question Helps

Finding the Christ in Ourselves

1. Why do we speak of "finding" the Christ in ourselves?

2. Explain how God lives and works.

3. How are you the Son of man? How the Son of God?

4. Why do we lose the consciousness of our spiritual identity?

5. How is Jesus the Elder Brother and Savior of humankind?

6. Explain how your body is "a temple of the living God." What takes place in a temple?

7. In what phase of our nature do truths have to be imbedded before they become for us living principles?

8. What is the distinction between a "reflection of God" and an "expression of God"?

9. Explain fully the "will of God."

10. Is salvation to be ours at some future time in a faraway place, or when it is acceptable? When are we really "saved"?

———————

Neither Do I Condemn Thee

1. Why is the "spoken word" regarded as having more power than the "unspoken word"?

2. What is the meaning of the word *criticize* as used here, and how is condemnation related to it?

3. What is "righteous judgment"?

4. Why should there be no condemnation of any person?

5. How does one work against God?

6. Explain: *"If you forgive the sins of any, they are forgiven; if you retain the sins of any, they are retained."* (John 20:23)

7. In the light of Jesus' teachings how can one handle the attitude of condemning another?

8. What causes a condemnatory attitude of mind?

9. How shall we rid ourselves of a condemnatory habit of mind? Explain the meaning of "habit."

10. How are we one with God and with one another?

In His Name

1. What is the purpose of a name?
2. What does God's name designate?
3. Explain the third commandment: *"You shall not take the name of the Lord your God in vain; for the Lord will not hold him guiltless who takes his name in vain."* (Exod. 20:7)
4. What is the meaning of I AM?
5. Why should one not use such phrases as "I am sorry" and "I am afraid"?
6. How do we ask "in His name"?
7. What did Jesus mean by the statement: *"Hitherto you have asked nothing in my name; ask, and you will receive, that your joy may be made full."* (John 16:24)
8. How can we tell whether or not we are using His name righteously?
9. Explain how all power is given to the Christ.
10. What is an "overcomer," and what is to be overcome?

Loose Him and Let Him Go

1. What fact seems particularly difficult for one person to remember in regard to another?

2. What is a sure sign of a free person?

3. How are you your "brother's keeper"?

4. What does proselyting mean? Why should one not be anxious about the welfare of another person?

5. What causes a person to seek that which is higher than he is today?

6. How do counselors and teachers often stand in the way of a student's attaining a desired consciousness?

7. To whom should each person turn for guidance?

8. What did Jesus mean when He said, "I am the way," and, "I am the door"?

9. Should the one who is apparently going wrong be specifically treated for his "sins"?

10. How do you "loose him and let him go"?

———————————

All-Sufficiency in All Things

1. What is it that is capable of supplying each person with the fulfillment of his own particular desires in abundant measure?

2. What do we mean when we speak of God "immanent" in us and in the universe?

3. What is divine substance, and what is its relation to manifest objects?

4. What is the Holy Spirit, and what is its relation to the Father, and to the Son, or Christ?

5. Explain how God is the supply and the supplier.

6. What governs the "shape" of our supply, and what fixes the "time" and the "quantity" of it?

7. Is it safe to teach that supply is a "gift" and that it does not depend only on the labor of head or hands?

8. What governs the outpouring of divine substance, and what inhibits its flow?

9. In its true sense, what is work?

10. From what phase of our being do we bring our world into manifestation?

God's Hand

1. What does the hand represent or symbolize?

2. Why does a person sometimes feel he is "empty-handed"?

3. Why do we say that man's hand represents the "hand of God"?

4. When do man's hands serve as the "hand of God"?

5. How did the woman cited in the text serve to bring freedom to a man?

6. Where does giving first take place?

7. Explain the phrase, "only say," and relate it to giving.

8. What is the relation between the "word" and the "hand"?

9. Of what is "giving" the natural outflow?

10. What blessings come to the one who serves as the "hand of God"?

———————

If Thou Knewest

1. Give a definition of the word *negation*, and show how it is used in this lesson.

2. Where does the belief in the "absence of good" exist?

3. Explain the meaning of the words *temporal* and *eternal*.

4. How would you help a dear one who appears to be "going wrong" and expresses unkindness?

5. How would you "heal" the suffering of poverty?

6. Explain how the condition of evil is a "delusion of the senses."

7. What is a gift, and what is the greatest "gift" to man?

8. What is grace, and how is God's grace manifested?

9. What is meant by "the deity"?

10. Explain the meaning of the Scripture: *"The Son of God was manifested, that he might destroy the works of the devil."*

———————

Trusting and Resting

1. What is meant by the statement, "holding to the Truth"?

2. What is a "treatment"?

3. What is it that heals all infirmities?

4. What is "tension," and what is its effect on yourself and others?

5. Where does your responsibility end and God's commence?

6. What part does praise have in spiritual treatment?

7. What has "time" to do with the answers to prayer?

8. What is the "stone" that is so great that is rolled away?

9. What is the "Lord" that is to be trusted implicitly?

10. What is peace, and how is the consciousness of peace attained by the individual?

————

The Spoken Word

1. Read Genesis 1 and John 1. To what phase of the creative process does each chapter refer?

2. To what do we refer when we write "word" with a capital "W"?

3. Name the days or steps in the creative process as given in Genesis 1 and 2, explaining the six days or periods of activity, culminating in the seventh day (step) or Sabbath. What follows these days or steps?

4. Why is it that our prayers are often just wishes?

5. What distinguishes man as the highest manifestation of God?

6. Why do we say that divine substance is forever "waiting for man"?

7. When man prays, does God "withhold" from him what is not for his good?

8. How does man "make" his body and his world?

9. What place in creation has thought? Where does the spoken word act?

10. What part does faith play in the process of bringing forth good in our lives? What other condition should be observed for perfect results?

———————

Unadulterated Truth

1. What is absolute Truth?
2. What is demonstration, and how is it made?
3. What is the primary cause of failure, poverty, sickness, death?
4. Explain each of the following terms: omnipresence, omnipotence, omniscience.
5. Explain "substance" and "life," and show how they are related to Spirit.
6. How may we be free from all undesirable conditions and circumstances?
7. What is meant by the statement, "There is no evil"?
8. When is anything "manifest"?
9. Why do we say that it is the spoken Truth that makes manifest?
10. Why is it necessary that we "realize" omnipresence?

———————

Oneness with God

1. Where and how is true prayer exercised?

2. What mental faculty is of prime importance in the exercise of true prayer?

3. How can we say that good is the only reality in the universe?

4. Explain the meaning of the word *fact* and what it is to "contemplate the facts of life from the highest point of view."

5. What is meant by "conscious oneness with the Father," and how is this conscious oneness attained?

6. Name some of the results that come from conscious oneness with God.

7. What is meant by "God's will" in you?

8. How do you "Have this mind in you, which was also in Christ Jesus"?

9. Explain the distinction between "revelation" and "inspiration" as used in this lesson.

10. How do you seek directly from the "Fountainhead," and how does its supply come to you?

Printed U.S.A.

12-F-8124-5M-1-86